EXAMINING RELIGIONS

St Mark's Gospel

David Adshead

HEINEMANN
EDUCATIONAL

Heinemann Educational,
a division of Heinemann Educational Books Ltd,
Halley Court, Jordan Hill, Oxford OX2 8EJ

OXFORD   LONDON   EDINBURGH
MELBOURNE   SYDNEY   AUCKLAND
IBADAN   NAIROBI   GABORONE   HARARE
KINGSTON   PORTSMOUTH NH (USA)
SINGAPORE   MADRID

First published 1990

British Library Cataloguing in Publication Data

Adshead, David
   St Mark's Gospel.
   1. Bible. N. T. Mark
   I. Title   II. Series
   226.306

   ISBN 0–435–30315–5

Designed and produced by Gecko Limited, Bicester, Oxon
Printed and bound in Great Britain by Butler & Tanner
Ltd, Frome and London

Acknowledgements

Acknowledgements are due to the following for
permission to reproduce photographs: Mike Abrahams/
Network p.45; Ancient Art and Architecture Collection/
Ronald Sheridan p.5; Andes Press Agency/Carlos Reyes
pp.7, 51, 61, 73; Associated Press Ltd pp.16, 42 (top);
Barnaby's Picture Library pp.27, 55 (right); Andrew
Besley, p.17; The Bridgeman Art Library pp.15, 31, 46;
British and Foreign Bible Society pp.64, 65, 94; John
Butterworth p.83; Church's Ministry among the Jews p.9;
Ray Dabrowski, Seventh Adventist Church p.55; Keith
Ellis Collection p.12; Glasgow Art Gallery and Museum
p.24; Sally and Richard Greenhill p.52 (left); Sonia
Halliday Photographs p.23, 32 42 (bottom), 58, 63; Robert
Harding Picture Library Ltd pp.69, 80 (left); Stephanie
Henry/Format p.52; Hutchinson Library p.6, 22, 26, 36,
90; Kobal Collection p.10; Mansell Collection pp.18, 21,
91; Popperfoto p.19; David Ridge Photography p.34; John
Sturrock/Network p.94 (bottom); Simon Warner p.80
(right); Zefa Picture Library (UK Ltd) p.8.

Cover photographs by: Ancient Art and Architecture
Collection (St Mark's Lion); The Bridgeman Art Library
(Chapel of Christ in Gethsemane, Coventry).

CONTENTS

1 INTRODUCTION

This book really consists of two books in one.

One is the Gospel of Mark, which was written over 1,900 years ago. It is reproduced in full, although not in order, and in a modern English translation rather than in the Greek in which it was originally written.

The rest of the book is intended to help you come to a thorough working knowledge and understanding of what Mark had to say.

It is a good idea to work through the book from beginning to end, unit by unit. This way it will be a bit like a guided tour. You will be introduced to things as and when you need to know them. You will gradually build up your understanding of what the Gospel is all about and you will be developing your critical (and theological!) skills.

There are two recurring topics and each has a unit devoted to it. One is 'Son of Man' and the other is 'Kingdom of God'. You can refer to these units earlier if you wish, but there is no need to. It is worth pointing out, however, that you will come across both phrases in Mark's Gospel well before you come to the units that deal with them.

When you have done this, it will be time to go through Mark's Gospel in the order in which he wrote it. Unit 37 has been designed to enable you to do this. This time, hopefully, you will be reading with understanding, realizing, for example, the importance of John the Baptist in identifying Jesus as the Messiah and appreciating that the idea of the suffering and death of Jesus is present at his baptism in what are only the opening verses of the Gospel.

Having said all this, however, it is also worth pointing out that, in common with the rest of the books in the *Examining Religions* series, it is quite possible to study each unit as a complete unit in itself.

The book assumes no previous knowledge on your part and it avoids technical theological language unless the meaning is carefully explained. Some of you with previous knowledge might find this a little tedious at times but please remember – patience is a virtue!

Having said that, the book tackles some very complex theological ideas as thoroughly as possible and is constantly trying to encourage you to develop your expertise.

If you are taking an examination at the end of your study – and most of you will be – it is very important to have a thorough factual knowledge of the Gospel itself. It is no use trying to talk about something you really know nothing about! At least you are dealing with a syllabus where everything is very clearly defined. No-one can add anything to Mark's Gospel – not before your examination anyway! That gives you a great advantage. The 'Quick quizzes' and the four 'Test yourself!' pages will help you to make sure you can remember the details accurately.

'For your folders' and 'Things to do' are designed to help you develop your skills of understanding and evaluation. You may find that you become quite involved in some of the suggestions – perhaps even too involved! In that case you may like to consider letting them become one of your coursework projects.

You will find a number of 'Coursework suggestions' on pages 92–94. These are all designed to reinforce your knowledge and understanding of the Gospel but also to show that Mark's Gospel is very much part of Christianity as a whole.

In fact, studying a Gospel is one 'way in', as it were, to studying the Christian religion. If you have no direct contacts with the Christian religion, it would not be a bad idea to try and make some. Find some friendly people, explain to them what you are doing, and ask them if they would be prepared to let you ring them up or go round and see them to talk through things discussed in the book.

It may not happen every day, or every week (they will be relieved to hear that!), but it is always useful to be able to talk to people involved in the religion about their views. You may find they disagree with what the book says. They may disagree with each other. It will certainly become a learning experience for them as well as for you and you will all enjoy it and benefit from it.

No Christian symbol is better known than the cross.

When you see it on a building, you can be fairly sure that Christians worship there. On a map it shows where you will find a church building. Priests, ministers and people all make the sign of the cross as a way of showing God's blessing. Archbishops and bishops wear one as a sort of badge of office. Organizations like the Red Cross use it to show that they stand for the relief of suffering. Lots of people who are not churchgoers wear a cross as a sort of charm and often – as in the films about Count Dracula – it has been regarded as an effective defence and protection against evil.

The cross became the 'official' symbol of Christianity when Christianity became the official religion of the Roman Empire. Christianity went on to become the framework for western culture, sharing all its success – and sharing too its sins and failures.

The shape of the cross being what it is, it has at times been difficult to tell it apart from the sword, and there are certainly some who wish that Constantine had never been converted!

In one sense, the cross stands for the very worst that people can do to each other. Crucifixion was arguably one of the most horrific forms of individual torture and death ever devised.

And yet, say Christians, Jesus accepted this as being – in the end – the only way to restore the broken relationship between God and his people.

He need not have been crucified; he need not have refused to answer Pilate; he need not have angered the High Priest; he need not have come to Jerusalem; he need never have left his job as a carpenter.

But then again, he knew all that. He was not stupid. Somehow, it seems from reading Mark's Gospel, he just *had* to do all these things.

Christians believe that having been alive in one place at one time, Jesus is now alive everywhere for all time. They say that because he suffered and died as he did, a new and better relationship has been made possible between God and his people.

And they go further. They say: for 'Jesus' read 'God'. In other words, it was God who took upon himself all the worst that people could do and be to each other in order to restore the broken relationship.

But all this is part of the development of Christian thinking. Mark's Gospel comes at a very early stage in that process. It says nothing, for example, about Jesus' birth or childhood. It begins when Jesus is already in his late thirties. And there, at his baptism, the voice from heaven identifies him as the Servant who is to suffer.

So we begin at what may appear to be the end. It is, however, where Christianity always has and always will begin – at the cross.

A Chilean crucifix

THINGS TO DO

▶ See how many different types of crosses you can find and try to discover what the various differences mean. Start with the plain wooden cross and the crucifix which are pictured on these pages. Now here are some names of the other styles you should be able to find:

Celtic
Coptic
Greek
Russian
St Andrew, St David, St George, St Patrick, etc.

A plain wooden cross

What follows is reckoned by most experts to be a very early Christian hymn. Paul quotes it in his letter to the Church at Philippi mid-way through the first century CE.

> *He always had the nature of God,*
> *but he did not think that by force he should try*
>   *to become equal with God.*
> *Instead of this, of his own free will he gave up all*
> *he had,*
> *and took the nature of a servant.*
> *He became like man*
> *and appeared in human likeness.*
>
> *He was humble and walked the path of obedience all*
> *the way to death –*
> *his death on the cross.*
> *For this reason God raised him to the highest place*
> *above*
> *and gave him the name that is greater than any*
> *other name.*
> *And so, in honour of the name of Jesus all beings*
> *in heaven, on earth, and in the world below*
> *will fall on their knees,*
> *and will openly proclaim that Jesus Christ is Lord,*
> *to the glory of God the Father.*

(Philippians 2:6–11)

3 FESTIVAL OR FUNERAL?

It was now two days before the festival of Passover and Unleavened Bread. The chief priests and the teachers of the Law were looking for a way to arrest Jesus secretly and put him to death. 'We must not do it during the festival,' they said, 'or the people might riot'.

(14:1–2)

Passover

The Jewish festival of Passover and Unleavened Bread is held every year in the early spring when the lambs are born and when, in Israel, the barley is being harvested. It is the time when Jews remember how God brought their ancestors out from slavery in Egypt.

For many years before Jesus was born and certainly until 70 CE, when the Temple was destroyed by the Romans, Passover was a pilgrim festival. According to Josephus, the first century Jewish historian, more than two and a half million Jewish people would travel to Jerusalem from all over the world each year. The city would be bursting at the seams for the week – just like Makkah is today when Muslims make their Hajj or pilgrimage.

During the day leading up to the Passover meal itself, all the old yeast would be burnt, and unleavened bread would be eaten for at least one week. Then, in the afternoon, in the Temple in Jerusalem, the lambs would be ritually slaughtered and their blood thrown in front of the altar by the priests. Later, their carcases would be roasted whole before being eaten with bitter herbs and unleavened bread at the Passover meal in the evening.

The Passover Story

Some 1,250 years before Jesus, the ancestors of the Jewish people, the Hebrews, were in Egypt. They had settled there many years before and for a while everything had gone well for them.

There came a time, however, when things began to go badly for Egypt and the Hebrews were blamed. They were forced into slavery for their Egyptian masters and their lives were made a misery. In addition, to try to keep down their numbers, a law was passed saying that all male Hebrew babies were to be drowned in the Nile.

It was at about this time that Moses was born. His mother hid him amongst the tall grass at the edge of the river in a watertight basket made of reeds and tar. His sister kept watch to see that he was safe. In fact, the Pharaoh's daughter came to the river to bathe and discovered the baby. She felt sorry for him and decided to take him back to the palace. His sister suggested that the princess might like to have a Hebrew woman to nurse him and Moses' own mother was given the job!

When Moses was a man, he became aware of how badly his own people were being treated. One day he saw an Egyptian kill one of the Hebrews and he

A Jewish family at the Passover meal

A Seder plate, used at the Passover meal

was so incensed that he killed the Egyptian. As a result he became a wanted man and the only thing he could do was run away. Eventually he settled in the land of Midian where he married the daughter of the priest and they had a son.

One day, when Moses was looking after his father-in-law's sheep and goats, he came upon a bush which was on fire but which was not being burnt up. A voice came from the bush, calling his name. Moses was convinced it was God who was speaking to him. God said he had decided to rescue his people and that Moses was to go to Egypt and bring them out to a land which God would make available for them.

After a great deal of persuasion, Moses went to Egypt with his brother Aaron, confronted the Pharaoh and demanded the release of the Hebrew people. Much as Moses expected, Pharaoh turned them down out of hand and then proceeded to make life even worse for the Israelite slaves.

So God gradually wore down Pharaoh's resistance with a series of ten plagues. First the Nile turned to blood, then the country was infested with frogs. Next there were gnats everywhere and after that, flies. All the Egyptian animals then died of a terrible disease, the whole population developed boils which quickly became open sores, and the crops were ruined by hailstorms. What was left was eaten up by a swarm of locusts. And as if that were not enough, there was total darkness for three days. With each plague, none of which affected the Israelites, Pharaoh's attitude softened, only to harden again once the plague had passed.

In the final plague, on a pre-determined night, God killed all the Egyptian first-born males. The Israelites had protected themselves by putting the blood of a lamb or a young goat all over their outside door frames. Before midnight, they ate the roasted meat with bitter herbs and with bread made without yeast. It was the first Passover. In the small hours of the morning Pharaoh was begging Moses and Aaron to take the Israelites away as soon as possible. They did not waste a minute.

By the time they reached the Red Sea, however, Pharaoh had yet again changed his mind. He sent the army after them to bring them back. But the story goes that God made the waters separate so that the Israelites could cross safely and then let them come back together to drown the Egyptian army.

God had brought the Israelites out of Egypt. Now he would lead them to Sinai to receive the Torah and then eventually to the land which he had promised them.

THINGS TO DO

▶ Find out what happens at a modern Jewish Passover Seder.

Who's Who

The priests looked after the Temple in Jerusalem and made all the sacrificial offerings which were required by the Torah (or Law). It was their job to maintain the ancient patterns of worship. They were by training (and often by nature) extremely cautious and conservative in their outlook and approach. Many of them were Sadducees (see unit 36).

The 'chief priests' probably means a leading group of priests made up of the High Priest, the ex-high priests and the members of those privileged families from which the high priests came.

The teachers of the Law were those who had studied the Torah in very great detail. They were experts in their field and few people, if any, were able to compete with their knowledge and understanding. For this reason many of them were members of the Sanhedrin, the Jewish Council. Most of them were Pharisees (see unit 31).

FOR YOUR FOLDERS

▶ Why do you think the chief priests and teachers of the law were so concerned to avoid a riot?

Preparing to Bury

Jesus was in Bethany at the house of Simon, a man who had suffered from a dreaded skin-disease. While Jesus was eating, a woman came in with an alabaster jar full of a very expensive perfume made of pure nard. She broke the jar and poured the perfume on Jesus' head. Some of the people there became angry and said to one another: 'What was the use of wasting the perfume? It could have been sold for more than three hundred silver coins and the money given to the poor!' And they criticized her harshly.

But Jesus said: 'Leave her alone! Why are you bothering her? She has done a fine and beautiful thing for me. You will always have poor people with you, and any time you want to, you can help them. But you will not always have me. She did what she could; she poured perfume on my body to prepare it ahead of time for burial. Now, I assure you that wherever the Gospel is preached all over the world, what she has done will be told in memory of her.'

(14:3–9)

The woman saw it as a way of showing how much Jesus meant to her. It was as if she were anointing him king in the ancient Jewish coronation ceremony (see unit 7). Jesus saw it not only as a very generous gesture on her part but also as a sign that his death was not far away.

People were angry, however, because they felt it was an extravagant waste of money when there was so much poverty in the world. The perfume would have cost a working person something like a whole year's wages.

Nard came from an Indian plant and in its pure form it was very expensive. Like myrrh, it was used to perfume dead bodies as well as living ones. It was often stored as an ointment in alabaster pots and is said to have kept its fragrance for several hundred years.

QUICK QUIZ

► Where was Jesus staying when the woman anointed him?
► What sort of jar was the perfume kept in?
► What else could she have done, according to some of the people there?
► How did Jesus describe what she had done?

'Preparing to bury'

Preparing to Betray

Then Judas Iscariot, one of the twelve disciples, went off to the chief priests in order to betray Jesus to them. They were pleased to hear what he had to say, and promised to give him money. So Judas started looking for a good chance to hand Jesus over to them.

(14:10–11)

FOR YOUR FOLDERS

First . . . work out your own answers to these questions:

▶ What do you think went through Judas' mind before he decided to go and see the chief priests?

▶ What do you think he said to them?

▶ Why do you think they were pleased to hear what he had to say?

▶ How important do you think the money was to Judas?

▶ Do you think that Judas saw what he was doing as betraying Jesus?

▶ Many people give one or more of three reasons for Judas doing what he did: that he was greedy; that he was ambitious; that he was making sure he finished up on the right side when the showdown came. Which of these, if any, do you think makes sense?

And now . . . discuss your ideas with your friends and work together to prepare a script for this particular scene. You will need to write parts for Judas and two chief priests at least. If you have a cassette recorder available, try recording the result and play it back to the rest of the group.

Preparing to Celebrate

On the first day of the festival of Unleavened Bread, the day the lambs for the Passover meal were killed, Jesus' disciples asked him: 'Where do you want us to go and get the Passover meal ready for you?' Then Jesus sent two of them with these instructions: 'Go into the city, and a man carrying a jar of water will meet you. Follow him to the house he enters, and say to the owner of the house: "The Teacher says, Where is the room where my disciples and I will eat the Passover meal?" Then he will show you a large upstairs room, prepared and furnished, where you will get everything ready for us.' The disciples left, went to the city, and found everything just as Jesus had told them; and they prepared the Passover meal.

(14:12–16)

It looks as if Jesus had made all the arrangements some time earlier. On a given day at a given time and just inside one of the gates of the city, the owner of the room would have arranged for a man to be carrying a jar of water. Male water-carriers usually carried leather bottles rather than stone pitchers. That was to be the tell-tale sign. Eventually the disciples would notice him, follow him and so find the house.

FOR YOUR FOLDERS

▶ Jesus went to great lengths to make sure that no-one else would know where they were going to be eating Passover. Why?

▶ This room seems to have remained the meeting place for Jesus' disciples for some while after his death and resurrection. It is very likely that it was part of the house where Mark himself lived (see Acts 12:12). Read Acts 1:12–26 to find out about one of the things which happened there and then answer this question: who replaced Judas?

The Disciples

When it was evening, Jesus came with the twelve disciples. While they were at table eating, Jesus said: 'I tell you that one of you will betray me – one who is eating with me.' The disciples were upset and began to ask him, one after the other: 'Surely you don't mean me, do you?' Jesus answered: 'It will be one of you twelve, one who dips his bread in the dish with me. The Son of Man will die as the scriptures say he will; but how terrible for that man who betrays the Son of Man! It would have been better for that man if he had never been born!' . . .

. . . Jesus said to them: 'All of you will run away and leave me, for the scripture says: "God will kill the shepherd, and the sheep will all be scattered." But after I am raised to life, I will go to Galilee ahead of you.' Peter answered: 'I will never leave you, even though all the rest do!' Jesus said to Peter: 'I tell you that before the cock crows twice tonight, you will say three times that you do not know me.' Peter answered even more strongly: 'I will never say that, even if I have to die with you!' And all the other disciples said the same thing.

(14:17–21 and 27–31)

There is nothing in Mark to suggest that this is *not* the Passover meal. On the other hand, he does not actually say that it *is* the Passover meal.

Jesus was quite clear in his own mind that he was going to die. He was also quite clear about the likely actions and reactions of his followers. Before the night was out, one of them was going to betray him; one of them was going to say that he had never known him; and all of them were going to run away and leave him.

A Free Church Communion – taking the bread . . .

. . . and the wine

The attitude of the disciples is interesting to say the least. When Jesus told them that one of them was going to betray him, they all said: 'Surely you don't mean me, do you?' This sounds as if each one of them was a bit unsure of his commitment to him.

But when Jesus told them that they were all going to run away and leave him – even to the point of denying they had ever known him – they all said they would rather die alongside him than do anything like that!

FOR DISCUSSION

▶ What do you make of the disciples' reactions?
▶ How might Jesus have replied, do you think, to the suggestion that he could have chosen his disciples more carefully?

The Last Supper

While they were eating, Jesus took a piece of bread, gave a prayer of thanks, broke it, and gave it to his disciples. 'Take it,' he said, 'this is my body.' Then he took a cup, gave thanks to God, and handed it to them; and they all drank from it. Jesus said: 'This is my blood which is poured out for many, my blood which seals God's covenant. I tell you, I will never again drink this wine until the day I drink the new wine in the Kingdom of God.'

(14:22–25)

Most Christians eat a piece of bread and many drink wine from a cup as part of their worship. It may not be every week. It may not be in every service. But, however and whenever they do it, they believe that they are taking part in something that goes right back through history to the last time that Jesus ate and drank with his disciples before his death. This action is therefore at the heart of Christian worship.

The service itself is known by a variety of names, depending on the particular type of Christian church or denomination. Divine Liturgy, Mass, Eucharist, Holy Communion, Lord's Supper, Breaking of Bread are among the most common titles.

All the New Testament writers agree that the first celebration took place on the evening before Jesus died. They also agree that Jesus was put to death at the time of the Jewish festival of Passover. Opinion is divided, however, as to whether the Last Supper was actually part of the Passover meal itself. It could have been just an ordinary evening meal at Passover time.

In any event, it offers a Christian re-interpretation of the Jewish meaning of Passover. Passover reminds Jewish people of their belief that they are part of the Israel (people of God) whom God set free from slavery in Egypt so that they could serve him in the world. Holy Communion reminds Christians of their belief that they are part of the new Israel which, through the death of Jesus, has been set free by God from slavery to sin to serve him in the world.

Christians have been divided since the Reformation in Europe in the sixteenth and seventeenth centuries over just what is meant by 'this is my body' and 'this is my blood'.

Catholic and Orthodox Christians take the view that although outwardly the bread and wine remain the same, the inward 'substance' actually changes to the body and blood of Jesus when the priest says the words which set them apart for this purpose in the service.

Most Protestants regard the bread and wine only as symbols and therefore speak of 'feeding on him by faith'.

All Christians believe that the living Jesus is present. They disagree on *how*.

New Covenant

Jesus says that his blood 'which is poured out for many . . . seals God's covenant'.

'Covenant' is the word which the Jews had used for hundreds of years to talk about the relationship which they had with God and which God had with them. It was more than simply an 'agreement' or a 'contract' between two parties. It involved the total and irrevocable commitment of the one to the other.

All the covenants had a sign to show that special promises had been made. In the one made with Noah it was the rainbow; with Abraham, the father of the Jewish people, it was circumcision; with the people as a whole it was the Law given to Moses at Sinai; and so on.

After the fall of Jerusalem in the sixth century BCE, the prophet Jeremiah said that God would make a new covenant. Christians believe that it began with Jesus and that its sign is the Holy Spirit.

Another word for covenant is 'Testament' – and that is why Christians call the Jewish Bible, which forms part of their own Bible, the 'Old Testament'. It is also why they call the Gospels, Letters and other books by Christian writers, which make up the rest of their Bible, the 'New Testament'.

In the language of the Bible, 'blood' means 'life'. So when Jesus talks about his blood, he is really talking about his life. It is the complete self-giving of Jesus in his life and his death which, for Christians, marks the starting-point of the new relationship.

THINGS TO DO

▶ Find out which Christian groups or denominations do *not* celebrate Holy Communion and why they do not.

▶ 'Holy Week' begins on 'Palm Sunday' and ends on Easter Sunday, when Christians celebrate the Resurrection of Jesus from the dead. 'Good Friday' is the name given to the day on which Jesus died. Find out the name of the day during Holy Week when most Christians celebrate the 'Last Supper' and why it is called this.

FOR YOUR FOLDERS

▶ Explain, in your own words, what Jesus meant when he said: 'This is my blood which is poured out for many, my blood which seals God's covenant.'

▶ What do you think Jesus meant when he said that he would not drink any wine again until he drank the new wine in the Kingdom of God?

13

6 AGONY AND ARREST

Mount of Olives

Then they sang a hymn and went out to the Mount of Olives.

(14:26)

The hymn which they sang could have been one of the psalms which are sung at the Passover meal.

The Mount of Olives is the hill to the east of Jerusalem, across the Kidron Valley and directly opposite the Temple. Jesus would have come and gone this way each day from Bethany where he was staying with friends.

Gethsemane

They came to a place called Gethsemane, and Jesus said to his disciples: 'Sit here while I pray.' He took Peter, James and John with him. Distress and anguish came over him, and he said to them: 'The sorrow in my heart is so great that it almost crushes me. Stay here and keep watch.'

He went a little farther on, threw himself on the ground, and prayed that, if possible, he might not have to go through that time of suffering. 'Father,' he prayed, 'my Father! All things are possible for you. Take this cup of suffering away from me. Yet not what I want, but what you want.'

Then he returned and found the three disciples asleep. He said to Peter: 'Simon, are you asleep? Weren't you able to stay awake even for one hour?' And he said to them: 'Keep watch, and pray that you will not fall into temptation. The spirit is willing, but the flesh is weak.'

He went away once more and prayed, saying the same words. Then he came back to the disciples and found them asleep; they could not keep their eyes open. And they did not know what to say to him.

When he came back to them the third time, he said to them: 'Are you still sleeping and resting? Enough! The hour has come! Look, the Son of Man is now being handed over to the power of sinful men. Get up, let us go. Look, here is the man who is betraying me!'

(14:32–42)

Gethsemane was on the other side of the valley from Jerusalem on the slopes of the Mount of Olives and probably quite close to the road to Bethany.

Jesus in Gethsemane,
Jesus praying more;
Cross is less than a day away,
Jesus praying more;
Can't go back now, the die is cast,
Jesus praying more;
Doesn't want to die at all,
Jesus praying more;
Fighting fear in agony,
Jesus praying more;
Seeking strength to stand the test,
Jesus praying more;
How to meet catastrophe,
Jesus praying more;
Trusting in his Father God,
Jesus praying more;
Puts himself in other hands,
Jesus praying more;
Finding perfect peace at last,
Jesus praying more;
Pulls himself up from the ground,
Jesus praying more;
Come what may he's ready now,
Jesus praying more.

QUICK QUIZ

▶ What did Jesus ask all the disciples to do in Gethsemane?
▶ What did he ask Peter, James and John in particular to do?
▶ What did he ask God to do?
▶ How many times did Jesus pray?
▶ Why were the disciples embarrassed?

FOR DISCUSSION

▶ Why do you think Jesus took just Peter, James and John with him rather than all the disciples?
▶ Why do you think Jesus was so upset?

Two things are clear from what Jesus said in his prayer. The first is that, like anyone else, he did not want to die. The other is that he could see that there was no avoiding it if he was going to do what he believed God wanted him to do.

Chapel of Christ in Gethsemane, Coventry Cathedral

FOR YOUR FOLDERS

▶ The word which Jesus used to address God was 'Abba', a word which a young child would have used to talk to his or her father, like 'Daddy' or 'Papa'. The early Christians followed Jesus' example in the way they said their prayers. Knowing this, what would you say Christians believe about God?

Arrest

Jesus was still speaking when Judas, one of the twelve disciples, arrived. With him was a crowd armed with swords and clubs, and sent by the chief priests, the teachers of the Law, and the elders. The traitor had given the crowd a signal: 'The man I kiss is the one you want. Arrest him and take him away under guard.'

As soon as Judas arrived, he went up to Jesus and said: 'Teacher!' and kissed him. So they arrested Jesus and held him tight. But one of those standing there drew his sword and struck at the High Priest's slave, cutting off his ear. Then Jesus spoke up and said to them: 'Did you have to come with swords and clubs to capture me, as though I were an outlaw? Day after day I was with you teaching in the Temple, and you did not arrest me. But the scriptures must come true.'

Then all the disciples left him and ran away.

(14:43–51)

Mark?

A certain young man, dressed only in a linen cloth, was following Jesus. They tried to arrest him, but he ran away naked, leaving the cloth behind.

(14:52)

Some people think this might have been Mark – a bit like the way in which Alfred Hitchcock wrote himself a very small part in each of the films he directed.

QUICK QUIZ

▶ Who did Judas bring with him?
▶ How did they know who to arrest?
▶ What happened to the High Priest's slave?
▶ When else could they have arrested Jesus?
▶ What did the disciples do?

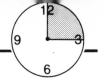
The 'Trial'

Then Jesus was taken to the High Priest's house, where all the chief priests, the elders, and the teachers of the Law were gathering. Peter followed from a distance and went into the courtyard of the High Priest's house. There he sat down with the guards, keeping himself warm by the fire. The chief priests and the whole Council tried to find some evidence against Jesus in order to put him to death, but they could not find any. Many witnesses told lies against Jesus, but their stories did not agree.

Then some men stood up and told this lie against Jesus: 'We heard him say: "I will tear down this Temple which men have made, and after three days I will build one that is not made by men."' Not even they, however, could make their stories agree.

The High Priest stood up in front of them all and questioned Jesus. 'Have you no answer to the accusation they bring against you?'

But Jesus kept quiet and would not say a word. Again the High Priest questioned him: 'Are you the Messiah, the Son of the Blessed God?'

'I am,' answered Jesus, 'and you will all see the Son of Man seated on the right of the Almighty and coming with the clouds of heaven!'

The High Priest tore his robes and said: 'We don't need any more witnesses! You heard his blasphemy. What is your decision?'

They all voted against him: he was guilty and should be put to death.

Some of them began to spit on Jesus, and they blindfolded him and hit him. 'Guess who hit you!' they said. And the guards took him and slapped him.

(14:53–65)

The Council (or Sanhedrin) consisted of about seventy people drawn from the great priestly families, the teachers of the Law and the elders.

Mark may have found out what went on in the Council from Joseph of Arimathea who was a member and who later buried Jesus' body (see unit 12).

As far as Mark is concerned, the whole thing was a complete fix. Questioning Jesus in the middle of the night only an hour or so after he had been taken into custody was suspicious to say the least. If justice is to be done, it is important that people should be regarded as innocent until they are proved guilty.

Jesus was assumed to be guilty from the start. The only problem the people had was finding some evidence on which to get him convicted.

To hold a formal trial the Council would have had to obtain permission from the Roman Governor. Such a trial would then have been subject to the Council's own rules which included the following:

- No trial to be held at night or on the eve of a feast.
- No sentence to be given on the same day as the trial.
- Trial to end if there were disagreement between witnesses.
- Anyone giving false evidence to receive the punishment for the alleged offence themselves.
- No prisoner to be condemned on own confession.

If it had been a formal trial, all these rules would have been broken. The religious authorities in Jerusalem were obviously very keen to get rid of Jesus.

The first clear accusation against Jesus was based on something which he said about the Temple. But elsewhere in the New Testament it is suggested that 'the temple Jesus was speaking about was his body' (John 2:21). Perhaps it was because of this that the witnesses were unable to 'make their stories agree'.

Eventually, on the basis of what Jesus said in reply to the High Priest, they found him guilty of blasphemy – which in this case meant that Jesus was claiming to be God. They agreed that he ought to be put to death.

Nelson Mandela as a freed man – was he wrongfully imprisoned?

Guilty or Not Guilty?

But was Jesus actually guilty of blasphemy?

In the underlying Greek, the High Priest's question used the phrase 'the Son of the Blessed One' – not 'God' as in the Good News Bible translation. This was very deliberate on the part of the High Priest because it *would* have been blasphemy if he had actually used the name of God. So he said 'the Blessed One' to avoid blasphemy. For his part, Jesus simply said 'I am'. On the face of it there is no blasphemy in this.

Nor was there any blasphemy in the idea of Jesus being 'Son of . . .'. In the Hebrew (or Aramaic) language which the High Priest would have used, this meant nothing more than someone having the sort of character which showed what God was like – a moral rather than a physical relationship.

It was when Jesus admitted to being Messiah – and the fact that he reinforced his claim by quoting scripture – that they knew they could get him put to death.

What he said did not amount to much more than: 'Yes, I believe I am the one whom God has been promising you.' Most people who claimed to be Messiah and whose followers joined them in armed rebellion finished up being crucified by the Roman occupying power. The leaders of the Council now had the means by which to dispose of Jesus. They could take him to the Roman authorities, accuse him of high treason and have him put to death – provided, of course, that he did not defend himself.

The story of the trial of Stephen, the first Christian martyr (Acts Chapters 6 and 7), is very similar. It was when Stephen said that he could 'see heaven opened and the Son of Man standing at the right-hand side of God!' that 'they all rushed at him at once, threw him out of the city, and stoned him' (Acts 7:56–58).

Messiah

'Messiah' is a Hebrew word which means 'Anointed One'. 'Christ' is the Greek word for 'Messiah'.

The anointing of kings and priests was a very ancient custom. It was the way Saul, David and Solomon, the first kings of Israel, had been 'crowned' a thousand years earlier.

To talk about the coming of an 'Anointed One' therefore was to talk about the coming of a king. It would mean national independence – a new God-given freedom.

The Messiah that most people hoped for was someone who would be born 'in David's line' – a political and military leader who would defeat the Romans. Under his rule they could look forward to the nation having a long and prosperous future. The whole thing would be God's doing.

QUICK QUIZ

- ▶ Where was Jesus taken after he was seized in Gethsemane?
- ▶ What did Peter do?
- ▶ What was the problem with the witnesses?
- ▶ Where did Jesus say he saw the Son of Man?
- ▶ How many of those present voted to say that Jesus was guilty and ought to be put to death?

THINGS TO DO

- ▶ Imagine that you are one of the high priests. Write a letter to a friend living in Rome describing what happened in the Council and what your feelings are about it.
- ▶ 'If Jesus is the Messiah, he is certainly not the sort of Messiah that most people are expecting.' You could imagine a TV news reporter saying that sort of thing after interviewing people like Judas, the High Priest and one or two members of the Council. Write the scripts of the interviews.
- ▶ Do you know of any trials today which in your opinion are examples of injustice? Give details.

Peter was still down in the courtyard when one of the High Priest's servant-girls came by. When she saw Peter warming himself, she looked straight at him and said: 'You, too, were with Jesus of Nazareth.'

But he denied it. 'I don't know . . . I don't understand what you are talking about,' he answered, and went out into the passage. Just then a cock crowed.

The servant-girl saw him there and began to repeat to the bystanders: 'He is one of them!' But Peter denied it again.

A little while later the bystanders accused Peter again: 'You can't deny that you are one of them, because you, too, are from Galilee.'

Then Peter said: 'I swear that I am telling the truth! May God punish me if I am not! I do not know the man you are talking about!'

Just then a cock crowed a second time, and Peter remembered how Jesus had said to him: 'Before the cock crows twice, you will say three times that you do not know me.' And he broke down and cried.

(14:66–72)

First

Simon Peter was the first in many ways.

He was the first to become one of Jesus' disciples (see unit 29); he was the first to recognize that Jesus was the Messiah (see unit 16); he was the first to stand up in public and speak about what Jesus meant to him (see Acts 2:14–42); and he was the first disciple to come back after they had all run away when he followed Jesus 'into the courtyard of the High Priest's house' (see unit 7).

Fool

And now, disaster of disasters, his accent gave him away and he became the first of Jesus' followers to claim that he knew nothing about him and had absolutely nothing to do with him.

The tradition is that Mark wrote down what Peter remembered about what Jesus had said and done (see unit 40). You can almost hear Peter telling this particular story and you can certainly feel the pain that it caused him to be reminded of it.

Peter denying Christ, by Carl Bloch

The Pope's Easter address to the crowds in St Peter's Square

Forgiven

John's Gospel (Chapter 21:15–19) has a story of how Jesus talked with Peter after his Resurrection. Jesus asks him three times whether he loves him and three times Peter says: 'You know that I love you.' At the end Jesus says: 'Follow me!' This is exactly what he had said when they had met for the first time three years earlier in Galilee. So Jesus is telling Peter to begin all over again, as if the denials had never happened. He has forgiven him for what he did.

Peter became the leading spokesman for the first Christians in Jerusalem. The tradition is that he later went to Rome where he became the first bishop of that Church. It is said that he was put to death by being crucified upside down during Nero's persecution of the Christians after the fire of Rome in 64 CE. The Roman Catholic Church regards all its popes as being the successors of Peter as Bishop of Rome.

QUICK QUIZ

► Who recognized Peter in the courtyard?
► What was he doing when this happened?
► What made the bystanders think he was one of Jesus' followers?
► What did Peter say God should do if he were not telling the truth?
► How many times did Peter deny that he knew Jesus?
► How many times did the cock crow?
► What did Peter do when he remembered what Jesus had said?

THINGS TO DO

► Imagine that the year is 42 CE. You have received a letter from the Christians in Rome asking for a character reference on a Simon Peter who has recently arrived there and who says that he is one of the earliest followers of Jesus. Write your reply.

Early in the morning the chief priests met hurriedly with the elders, the teachers of the Law, and the whole Council, and made their plans. They put Jesus in chains, led him away, and handed him over to Pilate. Pilate questioned him: 'Are you the king of the Jews?'

Jesus answered: 'So you say.'

The chief priests were accusing Jesus of many things, so Pilate questioned him again: 'Aren't you going to answer? Listen to all their accusations!'

Again Jesus refused to say a word, and Pilate was amazed.

(15:1–5)

Pilate's thoughts . . .

'It just doesn't add up. Why are they bringing me someone who says he's the Messiah? If they really believed it they'd be helping him and supporting him, not shopping him to me as fast as they can. Perhaps they've decided to support Roman rule in Palestine at last! No, I don't believe it – it's totally out of character. They obviously want to be rid of him, but goodness knows why. And there's no way I'm going to be able to find out if he won't talk to me. It's as if he wants to die . . . .'

Procurator and Province

Pontius Pilate became the Roman Procurator of Judaea in 26 CE. He normally lived at the headquarters at Caesarea on the Mediterranean coast, but during the Passover period he stayed in Jerusalem. The Roman garrison, which was housed in the Antonia Castle, right next to the Temple itself, would have numbered no more than 3,000 soldiers – about one soldier to every 900 people during the festival period.

The imperial government in Rome regarded Judaea as only a 'minor' province. That is why it was governed by a procurator rather than a legate or a prefect. It says something for the skill of those who were appointed that they managed to avoid civil war for sixty years. They probably did it – as Pilate does here – by being prepared to be leaned on rather than risk the lives of the Roman soldiers.

Judaea was not an easy province to rule at the best of times and because he did not even try to understand the religious feelings of the Jewish people, Pilate made many mistakes during his time there. Eventually, in 36 CE, he was ordered to Rome to explain why he had carried out a massacre in Samaria. Before Pilate arrived, The Emperor

Tiberius died and Pilate was never required to answer for what he had done. With great tact and diplomacy, however, the Roman authorities replaced him with someone else.

At every Passover festival Pilate was in the habit of setting free any one prisoner the people asked for. At that time a man named Barabbas was in prison with the rebels who had committed murder in the riot. When the crowd gathered and began to ask Pilate for the usual favour, he asked them: 'Do you want me to set free for you the king of the Jews?' He knew very well that the chief priests had handed Jesus over to him because they were jealous.

But the chief priests stirred up the crowd to ask, instead, for Pilate to set Barabbas free for them. Pilate spoke again to the crowd: 'What, then, do you want me to do with the one you call the king of the Jews?'

They shouted back: 'Crucify him!'

'But what crime has he committed?' Pilate asked.

They shouted all the louder: 'Crucify him!'

Pilate wanted to please the crowd, so he set Barabbas free for them. Then he had Jesus whipped and handed him over to be crucified.

(15:6–15)

FOR YOUR FOLDERS

▶ Write out the thoughts that might have gone through Pilate's head from the time when the people asked him for 'the usual favour' to the moment when he 'handed Jesus over to be crucified'.

Soldiers

The soldiers took Jesus inside to the courtyard of the governor's palace and called together the rest of the company. They put a purple robe on Jesus, made a crown out of thorny branches, and put it on his head. Then they began to salute him: 'Long live the King of the Jews!' They beat him over the head with a stick, spat on him, fell on their knees, and bowed down to him. When they had finished mocking him, they took off the purple robe and put his own clothes back on him. Then they led him out to crucify him.

(15:16–20)

The crowds called to Pilate for Jesus' death

It is almost as if the soldiers were following the Saturnalia rituals. This festival was celebrated in ancient Rome from the 17th to the 23rd of December. It was the season for a great deal of eating and drinking – just as it is today! There would be someone who would pretend to be a king and the slaves would get away with as much as they liked.

It was certainly an opportunity for these Roman soldiers to abuse a Jew who was about to be put to death for treason.

QUICK QUIZ

► What had Jesus been doing twelve hours earlier?
► What had the Council found Jesus guilty of?
► What did they accuse him of when they brought him to Pilate?
► How did Jesus respond?
► What was Pilate's reaction?
► Why did Pilate suggest he should set Jesus free?
► What was the reaction of the crowd?
► What sort of crown did the soldiers give Jesus?
► What did the soldiers do when they had finished mocking him?

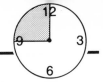

10 CRUCIFIXION

Simon

On the way they met a man named Simon, who was coming into the city from the country, and the soldiers forced him to carry Jesus' cross. (Simon was from Cyrene and was the father of Alexander and Rufus.)

(15:21)

Whether the sentence in brackets was originally written by Mark or whether it was added by a scribe producing a copy of the original does not really matter. Alexander and Rufus had become Christians by the time it was being written and were obviously well known to the readers. Their father would have been made to carry just the cross-piece for Jesus, not both pieces joined together.

Golgotha, traditional site of the crucifixion

Crucifixion

They took Jesus to a place called Golgotha, which means 'The Place of the Skull'. There they tried to give him wine mixed with a drug called myrrh, but Jesus would not drink it. Then they crucified him . . .

(15:22–24a)

Crucifixion was an extremely cruel form of torture which eventually led to death. It was used widely by the Romans as a way of punishing slaves, foreigners and the lowest class of criminal. No Roman citizen was ever crucified: it was beneath their dignity, whatever their crime.

The victim was attached to the cross-piece, sometimes by cords but more usually by nails. This was then lifted into place on the upright. There would be a peg for them to sit astride, which would relieve the strain on the nailed hands. The legs would then be held together at the ankles and turned round so that they could both be nailed to the upright with a single nail.

The cross was much lower than it often appears in Christian art. That way, the crucified person was much closer to the jeers and taunts of passers-by.

Eventually, the victims died through suffocation. Breathing became increasingly difficult. Often, their legs were broken to stop them lifting themselves up to get air into their lungs. To make sure the victims were dead, the executioners would often run a spear through them.

THROWING DICE

. . . and divided his clothes among themselves, throwing dice to see who would get which piece of clothing. It was nine o'clock in the morning when they crucified him. The notice of the accusation against him said: 'The King of the Jews.' They also crucified two bandits with Jesus, one on his right and the other on his left. (In this way the scripture came true which says: 'He shared the fate of criminals.')

(15:24b–28)

By putting the notice on the cross Pilate was in effect saying: 'This is what will happen to anyone who tries to lead a rebellion.'

JEERING

People passing by shook their heads and hurled insults at Jesus: 'Aha! You were going to tear down the Temple and build it up again in three days! Now come down from the cross and save yourself!'

In the same way the chief priests and the teachers of the Law jeered at Jesus, saying to each other: 'He saved others, but he cannot save himself! Let us see the Messiah, the king of Israel, come down from the cross now, and we will believe in him!'

And the two who were crucified with Jesus insulted him also.

(15:29–32)

Psalm 22

Mark had Psalm 22 very much in mind as he wrote these sections. The reason is that it seemed to have been uppermost in Jesus' mind (see unit 11).

The soldiers who guarded a cross had a right to keep the victim's clothes and they could well have decided who should have what by throwing the dice. Mark remembers verse 18 in the psalm:

> They gamble for my clothes
> and divide them among themselves.

And when the chief priests and the teachers of the Law start jeering at Jesus, Mark remembers verses 7 and 8:

> All who see me jeer at me;
> they stick out their tongues and shake their heads.
> 'You relied on the Lord,' they say.
> 'Why doesn't he save you?
> If the Lord likes you,
> Why doesn't he help you?'

Via Dolorosa, 'Way of Sorrows', the route to Golgotha

Christ of St John of the cross, by Salvador Dali

At noon the whole country was covered with darkness, which lasted for three hours. At three o'clock Jesus cried out with a loud shout: 'Eloi, Eloi, lema sabachthani?' which means 'My God, my God, why did you abandon me?'

Some of the people there heard him and said: 'Listen, he is calling for Elijah!' One of them ran up with a sponge, soaked it in cheap wine, and put it on the end of a stick. Then he held it up to Jesus' lips and said: 'Wait! Let us see if Elijah is coming to bring him down from the cross!'

(15:33–36)

Darkness

Unless it was a supernatural intervention, it is extremely unlikely that the three hours of darkness would have been caused by an eclipse of the sun. As Passover comes at the time of the full moon, such an eclipse ought to be impossible! It is more likely to be legendary, like the way in which the sun was said to have been darkened at the death of Julius Caesar and other similarly great people.

Certainly the idea of the darkness emphasizes the sense of separation from God.

There are only three occasions in Mark's Gospel when the actual Aramaic words which Jesus would have used are quoted. This is one of them. You will find the others in units 22 and 23.

Elijah

Some of the bystanders thought that Jesus had called for Elijah. There were many who thought that the great prophet would return before the Messiah came. If he were the Messiah, they thought that maybe they had better try to keep him alive in case Elijah did come. But the early Christians believed that Elijah had already come. (See unit 17 for more information on this.)

Psalm 22

As Jesus was dying on the cross, it seems that Psalm 22 kept going through his mind. It begins:

My God, my God, why have you abandoned me?
I have cried desperately for help,
but still it does not come.
During the day I call to you, my God,
but you do not answer;
I call at night,
but get no rest.

It goes on:

My strength is gone,
gone like water spilt on the ground.
All my bones are out of joint;
my heart is like melted wax.
My throat is as dry as dust,
and my tongue sticks to the roof of my mouth.
You have left me for dead in the dust.

But it ends:

All nations will remember the Lord.
From every part of the world they will turn to
him;
all races will worship him . . .

Future generations will serve him;
  men will speak of the Lord to the coming
    generation.
People not yet born will be told:
  'The Lord saved his people.'

The psalm begins with a cry of anguish but ends with great hope and confidence in the future. From feelings of absolute loneliness and dereliction, the psalmist comes through to the faith that God will eventually triumph. There are some who have come to the conclusion that Jesus died feeling utterly alone and abandoned by God. But most Christians believe that the words of Psalm 22 were on Jesus' lips as he died because they best expressed his feelings and his faith.

Death

With a loud cry Jesus died.

The curtain hanging in the Temple was torn in two, from top to bottom. The army officer who was standing there in front of the cross saw how Jesus had died. 'This man was really the Son of God!' he said.

(15:37–39)

According to Mark, the actual death of Jesus was mercifully quite sudden and not long and lingering like that of so many crucifixion victims.

QUICK QUIZ

- ▶ What time was it when Jesus gave his first loud cry?
- ▶ What does 'Eloi' mean?
- ▶ What did they offer Jesus to drink?
- ▶ What happened in the Temple when Jesus died?

Holy of Holies

The curtain in the Temple hung across the entrance to the innermost part which was called the 'Holy of Holies'.

Once every year (only on the Day of Atonement), one man representing everyone (the High Priest) went into the single most holy place (the Holy of Holies) carrying the blood of an animal as a symbolic way of offering the life of the people to God.

In the New Testament book called 'The Letter to the Hebrews', the writer suggests that by his death Jesus has done this, once, for all, and on a cosmic scale.

In other words, on one single and unique occasion in human history (the Crucifixion), Jesus became the representative of everyone (the High Priest) and went into the single most holy place (heaven itself) 'to remove sin by the sacrifice of himself'.

FOR YOUR FOLDERS

- ▶ 'The curtain in the Temple was torn in two, from top to bottom.'
  Do you see this as factual (what actually happened) or as theological (saying something about God and/or Jesus)?
  Give reasons for your answer.

Centurion

Mark finds a deeper meaning in what the centurion said. The officer was certainly impressed by the way Jesus had died, but what he said need not have meant anything more than that he was 'out of this world'. If he did mean it literally, he would probably have been talking about 'one of the (Roman) gods in human form'. What the Roman centurion said, without faith, is the sort of thing that Mark is hoping everyone will want to say, with faith.

Women Watching

Some women were there, looking on from a distance. Among them were Mary Magdalene, Mary the mother of the younger James and of Joseph, and Salome. They had followed Jesus while he was in Galilee and had helped him. Many other women who had come to Jerusalem with him were there also.

(15:40–41)

At 15:47 (see unit 12) Mark speaks of 'Mary the mother of Joseph'. At 16:1 (see unit 13) he speaks of 'Mary the mother of James'. Here, in 15:40, it says: 'Mary the mother of the younger James and of Joseph.' All it would need would be a copyist who thought the two James were the same person and v40 would be as good as written. At least, as in the case of Alexander and Rufus, the original readers would presumably know to whom Mark was referring.

12 BURIAL

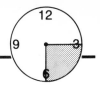

It was towards evening when Joseph of Arimathea arrived. He was a respected member of the Council, who was waiting for the coming of the Kingdom of God. It was Preparation day (that is, the day before the Sabbath), so Joseph went boldly into the presence of Pilate and asked him for the body of Jesus. Pilate was surprised to hear that Jesus was already dead. He called the army officer and asked him if Jesus had been dead a long time. After hearing the officer's report, Pilate told Joseph he could have the body. Joseph bought a linen sheet, took the body down, wrapped it in the sheet, and placed it in a tomb which had been dug out of solid rock. Then he rolled a large stone across the entrance to the tomb. Mary Magdalene and Mary the mother of Joseph were watching and saw where the body of Jesus was placed.

(15:42–47)

Burying the Crucified

The Torah says (Deuteronomy 21:22–23):

'If a man has been put to death for a crime and his body is hung on a post, it is not to remain there overnight. It must be buried the same day, because a dead body hanging on a post brings God's curse on the land.'

Josephus, the first century Jewish historian, wrote: 'The Jews are so careful about funeral rites that even criminals who have been sentenced to crucifixion are taken down and buried before sunset.'

There were some Jews who used to bury the bodies as a way of achieving religious merit. Joseph could have been one of these. He was not necessarily a follower of Jesus. In fact, he might even have been acting on behalf of the Jewish Council. Since they had demanded Jesus' death and were to that extent 'responsible' for it, they might have felt equally responsible for making sure that the law of the Torah was kept.

Graves were usually quite simple – holes dug in the ground with stones laid over them for protection. The richer and more important people would have their own (or they might share) burial chambers which were specially cut out of a rock face.

Temporary Arrangements

The Jewish Sabbath (or Rest-day) begins at sunset on Friday. That is why Joseph and the women were in a hurry to get the corpse buried. What they did was only a temporary arrangement. They would come back once the Sabbath was over to carry out a proper anointing and burial.

It seems likely that Joseph buried Jesus in what was to have been his own grave.

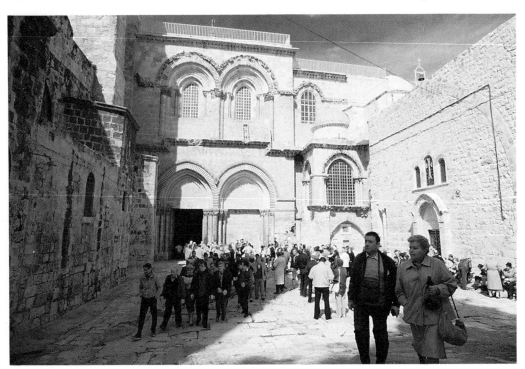

Church of the Holy Sepulchre, Jerusalem

Christian burial

THINGS TO DO

▶ Imagine that you are Mary Magdalene and describe what happened after the moment when Jesus died up to the point when Joseph rolled the stone across the entrance to the tomb.
Or . . .

▶ Imagine that you are Joseph and that you have finished burying Jesus' corpse. Write your report for the Jewish Council, detailing everything you have done since the moment Jesus died.

▶ There are 112 verses in Mark covering a twenty-four-hour period which begins with Jesus coming to the upstairs room with the disciples and ends with Joseph and the women burying his body. Starting at unit 6, take each three-hour period in turn (6 p.m.–9 p.m., 9 p.m.–12 p.m., 12 p.m.–3 a.m. and so on) and summarize *briefly* what happens in each.

QUICK QUIZ

▶ Where did Joseph come from?
▶ What was Pilate's reaction when Joseph asked for Jesus' body?
▶ What did Pilate do?
▶ What did Joseph buy?
▶ How did he secure the tomb?
▶ Who watched what he did?

13 WHAT'S MISSING?

The Empty Tomb

After the Sabbath was over, Mary Magdalene, Mary the mother of James, and Salome bought spices to go and anoint the body of Jesus. Very early on Sunday morning, at sunrise, they went to the tomb. On the way they said to one another: 'Who will roll away the stone for us from the entrance to the tomb?' (It was a very large stone.) Then they looked up and saw that the stone had already been rolled back. So they entered the tomb, where they saw a young man sitting on the right, wearing a white robe – and they were alarmed.

'Don't be alarmed,' he said. 'I know you are looking for Jesus of Nazareth, who was crucified. He is not here – he has been raised! Look, here is the place where they put him. Now go and give this message to his disciples, including Peter: "He is going to Galilee ahead of you; there you will see him, just as he told you."'

So they went out and ran from the tomb, distressed and terrified. They said nothing to anyone, because they were afraid.

(16:1–8)

No Proper Burial

Jesus' dead body was never anointed. All Joseph had done was to wrap it in a linen sheet and then put it in the tomb. As things turned out, the anointing at Bethany (see unit 4) really was an anointing for burial!

The three women who went to the tomb very early on the first day of the new week are the same three who helped Joseph put the body there on the Friday evening. The fact that they completely forgot that they would need some help with the stone may show just how anxious they were that Jesus should have a proper burial.

DISTRESSED AND TERRIFIED

Once inside the tomb, the women were confronted by what appeared to be a supernatural being who told them that Jesus had been raised and that he would meet them in Galilee, just as he had promised (see unit 5). It was obviously an extremely alarming experience because they ran out of the tomb, 'distressed and terrified'.

YOUNG MAN

What is interesting is the Greek word which Mark uses to describe the person they saw. Everywhere else it is used it means someone between twenty-five and forty years old – or, as it is translated here, 'a young man'. There are five other times when the word is used elsewhere in the New Testament and each time it is ordinary human beings who are being talked about.

Mark uses the word on one other occasion in his Gospel and that is when he describes the young man who ran away naked when they tried to arrest him along with Jesus (see unit 6).

QUICK QUIZ

► What did the women buy once the Sabbath was over?
► When did they go to the tomb?
► What did they say to one another on the way?
► What did they find when they arrived?
► Why did the women say nothing to anyone?

FOR DISCUSSION

► Who or what do you think the women saw?
► Why is it, do you think, that many Christians call Sunday 'the Lord's Day'?

Gospel Ending

In the earliest manuscripts the Gospel ends at the end of verse 8. The ending is so sudden that right from the first century, people have felt that the Gospel is unfinished.

They say it could be that Mark was interrupted as he was writing; that he was arrested and taken away to trial; that he was imprisoned or put to death or thrown to the lions or something and was never able to finish it.

But it could be that Mark did end his Gospel at that point. This is certainly not impossible, but it would mean there would be two things which would be regarded as odd.

The first is that the Gospel would end without any confirmation that Jesus had in fact risen from the dead. The situation would be that the body had gone missing and that the three women were running away in terror, having been told by a complete stranger that Jesus had been raised.

The second is that the last word of the Gospel in the original Greek is one which would never normally be used to finish a sentence. The word is 'because'. Mark's style is generally regarded as simple and direct, but he is not usually grammatically incorrect.

FOR YOUR FOLDERS

▶ 'Since Christians worship a living Jesus, there is no need for Mark to prove that Jesus rose from the dead.' Do you agree or disagree? Give reasons.

Attempted Endings

There were at least two attempts to write an ending for Mark's Gospel: a short one which was probably written before the end of the first century CE and a much longer one which comes from the second century CE. Both now appear as part of the Gospel.

THE SHORT ENDING

The women went to Peter and his friends and gave them a brief account of all they had been told. After this, Jesus himself sent out through his disciples from the east to the west the sacred and ever-living message of eternal salvation.

(16:9)

THE LONG ENDING

After Jesus rose from death early on Sunday, he appeared first to Mary Magdalene, from whom he had driven out seven demons. She went and told his companions. They were mourning and crying; and when they heard her say that Jesus was alive and that she had seen him, they did not believe her.

After this, Jesus appeared in a different manner to two of them while they were on their way to the country. They returned and told the others, but they would not believe it.

Last of all, Jesus appeared to the eleven disciples as they were eating. He scolded them, because they did not have faith and because they were too stubborn to believe those who had seen him alive. He said to them: 'Go throughout the whole world and preach the Gospel to all mankind. Whoever believes and is baptized will be saved; whoever does not believe will be condemned. Believers will be given the power to perform miracles; they will drive out demons in my name; they will speak in strange tongues; if they pick up snakes or drink any poison they will not be harmed; they will place their hands on sick people, who will get well.'

After the Lord Jesus had talked with them, he was taken up to heaven and sat at the right side of God. The disciples went and preached everywhere, and the Lord worked with them and proved that their preaching was true by the miracles that were performed.

(16:9–20)

THINGS TO DO

▶ Read the Resurrection stories in Matthew (Chapter 28), Luke (Chapter 24) and John (Chapter 20) and write your own summary of them in not more than 150 words.
▶ In what way(s) does your summary differ from the first half of the longer ending to Mark's Gospel (from 'After Jesus rose . . .' to '. . . will be condemned'?
▶ What conclusion can you draw about the longer ending?
▶ Read through the following passages and say which of the 'miracles' that are mentioned in the longer ending you are unable to find: Mark 9:38–39; Acts 2:1–13; Acts 28:1–9; 1 Corinthians 12:4–11.
▶ How do you explain the fact that the missing 'miracle' is missing not only from these passages but from the New Testament as a whole?

TEST YOURSELF!

1 Why is the symbol of the cross so important for Christians?

2 When did the chief priests and teachers of the Law start looking for a way to put Jesus to death?
3 At what time of the year is Passover celebrated?
4 What do Jews go without at Passover time?
5 What sort of animal was killed at Passover?
6 How did the earliest Christians use Passover to explain what the death of Jesus meant to them?
7 It is very unlikely that you would have found any Sadducees in the synagogues. Why?
8 How had the teachers of the Law come to know the Torah so well?
9 Why were the chief priests so concerned that the people should not riot?

10 What perfume did the woman use to anoint Jesus?
11 Why did some people get angry when she did it?
12 Why did Jesus think she had done it?
13 Who decided to betray Jesus to the chief priests?
14 How did the two disciples find out where they were to prepare the Passover?

15 What was it that Jesus said that made the disciples so upset while they were at table eating?
16 What did Jesus predict that Peter would do before the night was out?
17 What did Jesus say about the cup of wine from which they all drank?
18 Give one of the names by which this final meal between Jesus and his disciples is known.
19 What word did Jesus use to refer to the relationship of God with his people?

20 What was the name of the hill to which Jesus and the disciples went when they left the Upper Room?
21 What did Jesus say in his prayer in Gethsemane?
22 Why did the disciples 'not know what to say to him'?
23 What happened to the High Priest's slave when Jesus was arrested?

24 What did some men accuse Jesus of saying about the Temple?
25 What was it that Jesus said which made the High Priest accuse him of blasphemy?

26 What did the members of the Council do to Jesus after they had voted that he was guilty and should be put to death?

27 What does the word 'Messiah' mean?
28 What is there to suggest that Jesus was not guilty of blasphemy?

29 What was it that made the servant-girl so sure that Peter was one of Jesus' followers?
30 How did Peter react when the cock crowed a second time?
31 What happened to Peter later on in the early Church?

32 What question did Pilate ask Jesus?
33 What answer did Jesus give?
34 Why was Barabbas in prison?
35 What did the soldiers do to Jesus before they led him out to crucify him?

36 Who was forced to carry Jesus' cross?
37 What was Jesus offered before he was crucified?
38 How did the soldiers decide who should have which piece of Jesus' clothing?
39 What did the chief priests and teachers of the Law say to each other when they jeered at Jesus on the cross?

40 What was going through Jesus' mind as he hung on the cross?
41 Who did they think he was calling for?
42 What did the army officer say when he saw how Jesus had died?
43 Name one of the women watching.

44 Who asked Pilate for the body of Jesus?
45 Why might he have done this?

46 Who did the women find in the tomb on the Sunday morning?
47 What was the message for Peter and the disciples?
48 How did the women react?

49 Why did people think that Mark's Gospel was not finished?
50 What did they do about it?

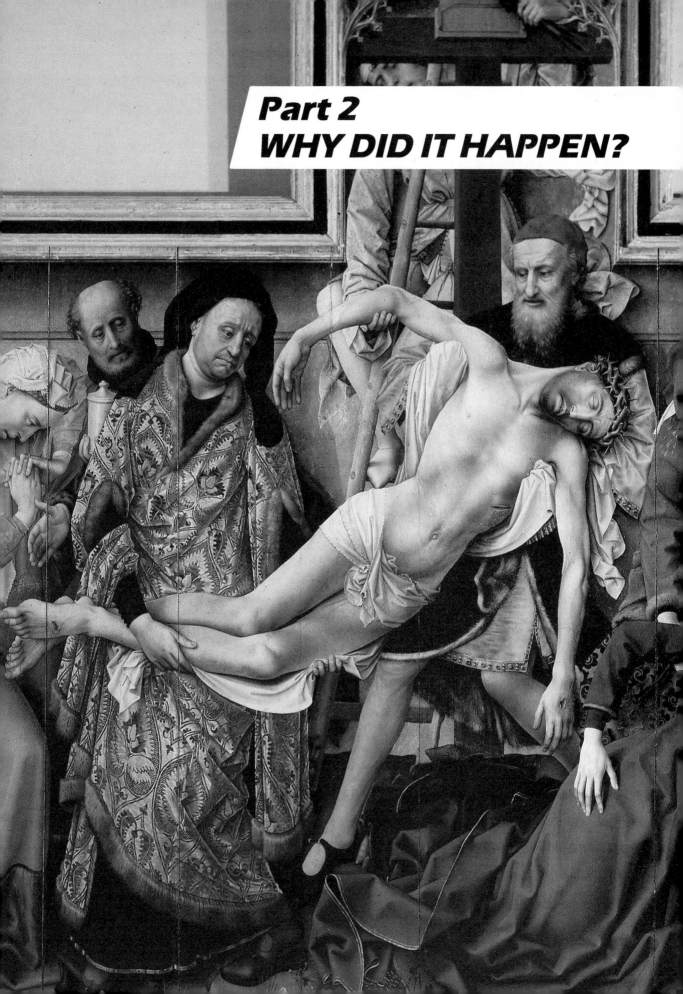

Who would have believed what we now report?
    Who could have seen the Lord's hand in this?
It is the will of the Lord that his servant
    should grow like a plant taking root in dry ground.
He had no dignity or beauty
    to make us take notice of him.
There was nothing attractive about him,
    nothing that would draw us to him.
We despised him and rejected him;
    he endured suffering and pain.
No-one would even look at him –
    we ignored him as if he were nothing.
But he endured the suffering which should have
    been ours, the pain that we should have borne.
All the while we thought that his suffering
    was punishment sent by God.
But because of our sins he was wounded,
    beaten because of the evil we did.
We are healed by the punishment he suffered,
    made whole by the blows he received.
All of us were like sheep that were lost,
    each of us going his own way.
But the Lord made the punishment fall on him,
    the punishment all of us deserved.
He was treated harshly, but endured it humbly;
    he never said a word.

Like a lamb about to be slaughtered, like a sheep
    about to be sheared, he never said a word.
He was arrested and sentenced and led off to die,
    and no-one cared about his fate.
He was put to death for the sins of our people.
He was placed in a grave with evil men,
    he was buried with the rich,
    even though he had never committed a crime or
    ever told a lie.

It was my will that he should suffer;
    his death was a sacrifice to bring forgiveness.
And so he will see his descendants;
    he will live a long life,
    and through my purpose will succeed.
After a life of suffering, he will again have joy;
    he will know that he did not suffer in vain.
My devoted servant with whom I am pleased, will
    bear the punishment of many
    and for his sake I will forgive them.
And so I will give him a place of honour,
    a place among great and powerful men.
He willingly gave his life
    and shared the fate of evil men.
He took the place of many sinners
    and prayed that they might be forgiven.

(Isaiah 53:1–12)

'. . . grow like a plant taking route in dry ground . . .'

The Servant

The quotation opposite is one of the so-called 'Servant Songs' from the book of Isaiah. Most experts agree that they were originally written when the capital Jerusalem had been destroyed by the Babylonian armies, when the nation of Israel had ceased to exist, and when most of the people living there had been deported to Babylon. All this happened in the sixth century BCE.

Most thinking people eventually accepted the idea that the nation had deserved this sort of punishment for having been unfaithful and disobedient towards God.

But the suffering which the Servant endured was *undeserved* suffering. He entered into it willingly, accepting that through it, God's forgiveness would be brought to many people. It was by his suffering and death that things were going to be put right.

WHO IS THE SERVANT?

There can be no doubt that, for the first Christians, *Jesus* was the Servant.

But whose idea was it?

Did things just happen in the way they did? Did someone then realize that the way things had turned out was very similar to the Servant Songs? And did that someone then suggest that Jesus could have been a Servant-Messiah? In other words, did Christianity begin because some unknown person had deep insight into the meaning and significance of these ideas in Isaiah?

Or did things happen in the way they did because Jesus made them happen in that way? Did he deliberately use the Servant Songs as a sort of script which he was to follow? Was he in fact setting out to show by all his words and actions that he was the Servant-Messiah? In other words, did Christianity begin because Jesus himself had this deep insight into the meaning and significance of these ideas in Isaiah?

FOR DISCUSSION

▶ Which of the above two interpretations do you think Christians would prefer? Why?

FOR YOUR FOLDERS

▶ In what ways *does* this Servant Song paint a picture of Jesus?
▶ In what ways does this Servant Song *not* paint a picture of Jesus?
▶ It seems that very often an innocent person has to suffer before things are put right for others. How true do you think this is? Give examples in support of your answer.

15 THE SON OF MAN

'Son of Man' is the literal Greek translation of the Hebrew/Aramaic phrase 'Bar nasha' which could mean:

● Any person (humanity in general); or
● *This* person (= me, as in 'one' or 'I'); or
● *The person* (a title for the Messiah).

The phrase occurs fourteen times in Mark's Gospel and all fourteen are set out below.

'Self portrait'

1 *(Jesus said) . . . 'I will prove to you, then, that the Son of Man has authority on earth to forgive sins.' So he (Jesus) said to the paralyzed man . . .* (2:10)

2 *And Jesus concluded: 'The Sabbath was made for the good of man; man was not made for the Sabbath. So the Son of Man is Lord even of the Sabbath.'* (2:27–28)

3 *Then Jesus began to teach his disciples: 'The Son of Man must suffer much and be rejected . . . put to death, but . . . rise to life.'* (8:31)

4 *Jesus . . . told them . . . 'If a person is ashamed of me and of my teaching in this godless and wicked day, then the Son of Man will be ashamed of him when he comes in the glory of his Father with the holy angels.'* (8:38)

5 *As they came down the mountain, Jesus ordered them: 'Don't tell anyone what you have seen, until the Son of Man has risen from death.'* (9:9)

6 *(Jesus said) . . . 'Why do the scriptures say that the Son of Man will suffer much and be rejected?'* (9:12)

7 *. . . Jesus was teaching his disciples: 'The Son of Man will be handed over to men who will kill him. Three days later, however, he will rise to life.'* (9:31)

8 *'Listen', Jesus told them, 'we are going up to Jerusalem where the Son of Man will be handed over to the chief priests and the teachers of the Law . . .'* (10:33)

9 *(Jesus said) . . . 'The Son of Man did not come to be served; he came to serve and to give his life to redeem many people.'* (10:45)

10 *(Jesus said) . . . 'Then the Son of Man will appear, coming in the clouds with great power and glory.'* (13:26)

11 *(Jesus said) . . . 'The Son of Man will die as the scriptures say he will; but how terrible for*

12 *that man who betrays the Son of Man!'* (14:21)

13 *(Jesus said) . . . 'The hour has come! Look, the Son of Man is now being handed over to the power of sinful men . . .'* (14:41)

14 *'I am (the Messiah),' answered Jesus, 'and you will all see the Son of Man seated on the right of the Almighty and coming with the clouds of heaven.'* (14:62)

THINGS TO DO

▶ Write out a list 1–14.

▶ Draw three columns, like those below. Head the first 'Anyone', the second 'I/Me' and the third 'The Messiah'. Work through the following quotations, one by one, and decide which of the three meanings fits the phrase 'Son of Man' best. Put a tick under the relevant column alongside the quotation's number. You will probably need to tick more than one column.

	Anyone	I/Me	The Messiah
1			
2			
3			

In other words, at the time that Daniel was written, the phrase would have come under column 1, but by the time Mark was written, it had become a title for the Messiah – definitely column 3.

Messianic Title

So when did this change take place?

The answer depends on when another book, called the 'Similitudes of Enoch', was written. In this book the phrase 'Son of Man' is quite clearly being used as a Messianic title. The result would be a sort of 'knock-on' effect as far as the book of Daniel is concerned. Most experts (the majority) say the Similitudes were written in the first century BCE; some (the minority) say the first century CE.

The majority think Jesus took what was a little known Messianic title at the time and made it his own by pouring into it his own understanding of what it meant to be Messiah (that is, the idea of the 'suffering servant').

The minority think that Mark took what had recently become a Messianic title and used it in his Gospel as a way of claiming Messiahship for Jesus.

FOR DISCUSSION

▶ Who do you agree with – the majority, the minority or neither? Why?

Results

You will probably find that you have only one or two ticks under the first column, most (perhaps all) of them ticked under the second column, and all (possibly most) of them ticked under the third column.

This makes it clear that:

a) 'Son of Man' is a title for the Messiah; and

b) Jesus is saying, in effect, 'I am the Messiah'.

Does this mean, then, that he was breaking his own rule of secrecy? The answer is probably 'no'. It would depend on whether or not 'Son of Man' was recognized as a Messianic title by those who were listening to him.

If you look up what is being quoted in number 14 (Daniel 7:13) you will find it says: '. . . I saw what looked like a human being . . .'

The Crucifixion is usually reckoned to have taken place in about 29/30 CE. It is unlikely that Mark's Gospel, the earliest of the four, was written before 65 CE (see unit 40).

So there is a period of something like thirty-five years when there were no written Gospels.

Most of Paul's letters were written during this period but the earliest is not likely to have been written before 48/49 CE.

That leaves about eighteen/twenty years for which we have no direct evidence other than the stories, traditions and legends which make up the first twelve chapters of the Acts of the Apostles.

To judge by these, it was a period in which the followers of Jesus were pressing his claim to be Messiah among their fellow Jews in the synagogues of the Roman world – with varying degrees of success.

Early Christian Preaching

It seems that the early Christian preachers were saying something along these lines:

- First – 'The Messiah had to suffer and die and rise again. Jesus has shown us that this is in fact what the scriptures are saying.'
- Second – 'Jesus of Nazareth has suffered and died and risen again. We can bear witness to this.'
- Third – 'It follows that Jesus of Nazareth is the Messiah; and if you believe that – as you should – you will need to make big changes to your lifestyle.'

In saying this, of course, they were offering someone who on the face of it might have seemed like a loser.

The preaching about Jesus still goes on all over the world

WHOSE IDEA WAS IT?

There seems little doubt that as Jesus had studied the scriptures, he had come to two inescapable conclusions. One was that the Messiah *had* to suffer. The other was that *he* was that Messiah.

So this was what he kept on explaining to his disciples. During his lifetime they were reluctant to accept what he said – just like the Jews in the synagogues around the Mediterranean later. They all had their own ideas about what a Messiah should be like and they each tried to persuade Jesus that they were right and he was wrong.

It was not until after his death and resurrection, perhaps, that they realized that he was right and they were wrong. Everything he had said during his life began to make sense. They were then convinced – at least enough to try to persuade all their fellow Jews – which meant being prepared to suffer and die in the same way as Jesus.

The Necessity of Suffering

Then Jesus and his disciples went away to the villages near Caesarea Philippi. On the way he asked them: 'Tell me, who do people say I am?' 'Some say that you are John the Baptist,' they answered, 'others say that you are one of the prophets.'
'What about you?' he asked them. 'Who do you say I am?'
Peter answered: 'You are the Messiah.'
Then Jesus ordered them: 'Do not tell anyone about me.' Then Jesus began to teach his disciples: 'The Son of Man must suffer much and be rejected by the elders, the chief priests, and the teachers of the Law. He will be put to death, but three days later he will rise to life.' He made this very clear to them. So Peter took him aside and began to rebuke him. But Jesus turned round, looked at his disciples, and rebuked Peter. 'Get away from me, Satan,' he said. 'Your thoughts don't come from God but from Man!'

(8:27–33)

Jesus and his disciples left that place and went on through Galilee. Jesus did not want anyone to know where he was, because he was teaching his disciples: 'The Son of Man will be handed over to men who will kill him. Three days later, however, he will rise to life.'

But they did not understand what this teaching meant, and they were afraid to ask him.

(9:30–32)

Jesus and his disciples were now on the road going up to Jerusalem. Jesus was going ahead of the disciples, who were filled with alarm; the people who followed behind were afraid. Once again Jesus took the twelve disciples aside and spoke of the things that were going to happen to him. 'Listen,' he told them, 'we are going up to Jerusalem where the Son of Man will be handed over to the chief priests and the teachers of the Law. They will condemn him to death and then hand him over to the Gentiles, who will mock him, spit on him, whip him, and kill him; but three days later he will rise to life.'

(10:32–34)

FOR DISCUSSION

▶ Was Jesus the Messiah because he suffered and died or did he suffer and die because he was the Messiah?

QUICK QUIZ

▶ Where were they when Jesus asked his disciples who people said he was?
▶ Who did Peter say Jesus was?
▶ What title did Jesus use to talk about himself?
▶ What did Jesus say was going to happen to him?

Caesarea Philippi

Caesarea Philippi was about twenty-four miles north of the Sea of Galilee in the foothills of Mount Hermon. It had recently been rebuilt by Philip, the tetrarch of Ituraea. He named it Caesarea in honour of the Emperor Augustus and Philippi (Philip's) to distinguish it from the Caesarea on the Mediterranean coast.

Mark was probably writing with the benefit of hindsight when it came to filling in the fine details about what Jesus expected to happen when he arrived at Jerusalem.

What People Thought About Jesus

That Jesus was offering a new way of looking at what the scriptures had to say seems fairly clear by the way in which some people at least were saying that he was 'one of the prophets'.

That he was fairly forthright and revolutionary in his approach is confirmed by the way in which some people thought he was John the Baptist come back from the dead (see unit 17).

That he was very close to being the Messiah in some people's eyes is clear from the fact that some of them thought he was Elijah, who was due to return before the Messiah actually came (see unit 17).

And even though those closest to him, like Peter, firmly believed he was the Messiah, they had not even begun to understand what he meant when he talked about the need for suffering and death – 'and they were afraid to ask him'.

Peter's Challenge

At one point, Peter was quite prepared to challenge him on it, even contradict him. Jesus called him Satan because traditionally Satan was the one who tested the extent of people's commitment. But he found that Jesus was determined to do it – nothing would shake him. The popular ideas about the Messiah were 'men's thoughts'. The ideas which Jesus found in Isaiah about a suffering Servant-Messiah were 'God's thoughts'.

FOR YOUR FOLDERS

▶ Jesus' request that his disciples should keep secret the fact of his being Messiah is one of the keynotes of Mark's Gospel. Why do you think Jesus insisted on such secrecy?

It began as the prophet Isaiah had written:

'God said: "I will send my messenger ahead of you to clear the way for you."
Someone is shouting in the desert:
"Get the road ready for the Lord;
make a straight path for him to travel!"'

So John appeared in the desert, baptizing and preaching. 'Turn away from your sins and be baptized,' he told the people, 'and God will forgive your sins.' Many people from the province of Judaea and the city of Jerusalem went out to hear John. They confessed their sins, and he baptized them in the River Jordan.

John wore clothes made of camel's hair, with a leather belt round his waist, and his food was locusts and wild honey. He announced to the people: 'The man who will come after me is much greater than I am. I am not good enough even to bend down and untie his sandals. I baptize you with water, but he will baptize you with the Holy Spirit.'

(1:2–8)

Now King Herod heard about all this, because Jesus' reputation had spread everywhere. Some people were saying: 'John the Baptist has come back to life! That is why he has this power to perform miracles.'

Others, however, said: 'He is Elijah.'

Others said: 'He is a prophet, like one of the prophets of long ago.'

When Herod heard it, he said: 'He is John the Baptist! I had his head cut off, but he has come back to life!' Herod himself had ordered John's arrest, and he had him chained and put in prison. Herod did this because of Herodias, whom he had married, even though she was the wife of his brother Philip. John the Baptist kept telling Herod: 'It isn't right for you to be married to your brother's wife!'

So Herodias held a grudge against John and wanted to kill him, but she could not because of Herod. Herod was afraid of John because he knew that John was a good and holy man, and so he kept him safe. He liked to listen to him, even though he became greatly disturbed every time he heard him.

Finally Herodias got her chance. It was on Herod's birthday, when he gave a feast for all the chief government officials, the military commanders, and the leading citizens of Galilee. The daughter of Herodias came in and danced, and pleased Herod and his guests. So the king said to the girl; 'What would you like to have? I will give you anything you want.' With many vows he said to her: 'I swear that I will give you anything you ask for, even as much as half my kingdom!'

So the girl went out and asked her mother: 'What shall I ask for?' 'The head of John the Baptist,' she answered. The girl hurried back at once to the king and demanded: 'I want you to give me here and now the head of John the Baptist on a dish!'

This made the king very sad, but he could not refuse her because of the vows he had made in front of all the guests. So he sent off a guard at once with orders to bring John's head. The guard left, went to the prison, and cut John's head off; then he brought it on a dish and gave it to the girl, who gave it to her mother. When John's disciples heard about this, they came and took away his body, and buried it.

(6:14–29)

They obeyed his order (not to tell anyone what they had seen), but among themselves they started discussing the matter. 'What does this "rising from death" mean?' And they asked Jesus: 'Why do the teachers of the Law say that Elijah has to come first?'

His answer was: 'Elijah is indeed coming first in order to get everything ready. Yet why do the scriptures say that the Son of Man will suffer much and be rejected? I tell you, however, that Elijah has already come and that people treated him just as they pleased, as the scriptures say about him.'

(9:10–13)

QUICK QUIZ

▶ Where did people come from to hear John the Baptist?
▶ Whose prophecy does Mark quote?
▶ Where was John baptizing and preaching?
▶ Who did Herod think John was?
▶ In what way had John criticized Herod?
▶ Why was it that Herodias had not been able to get John killed before this?
▶ Who was expected to return before the Messiah came?

Elijah Returns

Malachi, a Jewish prophet who lived about 450 years before Jesus, predicted that the prophet Elijah, who had been 'taken up from the earth' would come back before the Messiah himself came. Malachi's words were taken seriously. They were already regarded as being part of the scriptures. So then, if Jesus was the Messiah, who was Elijah? Mark said he was John the Baptist – and he gave what amounts to three reasons.

JOHN LOOKED LIKE ELIJAH

The story goes (2 Kings 1:2–8) that about 850 years before the time of Jesus, the Israelite King Ahaziah had been seriously injured in a fall from the palace balcony. He sent messengers to ask at the shrine of a foreign god whether he would recover. On their way the messengers met a man who told them that if the king were to ask his own God, the answer would be that he was not going to recover from his injuries – in fact, he was going to die!

'What did the man look like?' the king asked.

'He was wearing a cloak made of animal skins, tied with a leather belt,' they answered.

'It's Elijah!' the king exclaimed.

JOHN BEHAVED LIKE ELIJAH

(You will need to read 1 Kings 21:1–24)

In this story, the three main characters are King Ahab, Queen Jezebel and Elijah. In the story from Mark's Gospel it is as if all three have simply changed their names to King Herod, Queen Herodias and John the Baptist. The plot may be different but it is basically still the same battle between good and evil which is going on.

In the first story Elijah is the winner and Jezebel the loser. Eight and a half centuries later Jezebel (or Herodias) is the winner and this time Elijah is the loser. But Elijah (or John the Baptist) is still the prophet who speaks out fearlessly and criticizes the king for his behaviour. The marriage was against Jewish Law (see Leviticus 18:16).

JOHN DID WHAT ELIJAH WOULD DO

In Chapter 1:2–8 Mark has brought together two other prophecies which appear to have come true – one from Malachi and the other from Isaiah. Both seem to be saying that someone will prepare the way for the Messiah. John confirms this is what he is doing.

Baptism

The word 'baptism' actually means 'washing'. By washing the whole body in running water, John was asking people to show they were sorry about how they had behaved, that they were asking God to forgive them for what they had done and were making a completely fresh start.

Theoretically there was no reason why a person could not be baptized every day to show how they felt. In monastic communities like the one at Qumran there appear to have been regular ritual washings. It is for this reason that some people have tried to connect John with this sort of sect.

By contrast, Christian baptism is regarded by most Christians as a once-for-all event.

Most Churches baptize children. This is often called 'christening'. When they grow up they are 'confirmed' in their Christianity in a ceremony called 'confirmation'.

Some Christian denominations like the Baptists refuse to baptize young children. They have a ceremony called 'Believer's baptism' which symbolizes the fact that a person has died to their old life and has risen again to start a completely new life as a Christian.

As they approached Jerusalem, near the towns of Bethphage and Bethany, they came to the Mount of Olives. Jesus sent two of his disciples on ahead with these instructions: 'Go to the village there ahead of you. As soon as you get there, you will find a colt tied up that has never been ridden. Untie it and bring it here. And if someone asks you why you are doing that, tell him that the Master needs it and will send it back at once.'

So they went and found a colt out in the street, tied to the door of a house. As they were untying it, some of the bystanders asked them: 'What are you doing, untying that colt?'

They answered just as Jesus had told them, and the men let them go . . . .

(11:1–6)

THINGS TO DO

▶ There are two extracts set out below. One is from the book of Zechariah, who was one of the prophets, and the other is from a psalm, one of the Jewish religious songs. Read them both carefully and when you have done this, write a conclusion for Mark 11:1–6 (see above), using no more than about 100 words.

Rejoice, rejoice, people of Zion!
Shout for joy, you people of Jerusalem!
Look, your king is coming to you!
He comes triumphant and victorious,
but humble and riding on a donkey –
on a colt, the foal of a donkey.
The Lord says:
'I will remove the war-chariots from Israel
and take the horses from Jerusalem;
the bows used in battle will be destroyed.
Your king will make peace among the nations;
he will rule from sea to sea,
from the River Euphrates to the ends of the earth.'
(Zechariah 9:9–10)

May God bless the one who comes in the name of the Lord!
From the Temple of the Lord we bless you.
The Lord is God; he has been good to us.
With branches in your hands, start the festival and march round the altar.
You are my God, and I will give you thanks;
I will proclaim your greatness.
(Psalm 118:26–28)

THINGS TO DO

▶ Now read Mark 11:7–11 in your bible and answer the following questions:
a Do you think that Jesus quite deliberately acted out Zechariah's prophecy to make it clear that he was a Messiah of peace and not a freedom-fighter?
b Or do you think that Mark quite deliberately used Zechariah's prophecy and made up a story to make it clear that Jesus was a Messiah of peace and not a freedom-fighter?
Give reasons for your answer.

▶ Christians celebrate Jesus' entry into Jerusalem on Palm Sunday, a week before Easter Sunday. They sing special hymns and follow special customs on this day. Find out what these are.

FOR YOUR FOLDERS

▶ The Law, the Prophets and the Writings (the Jewish Bible) were *the Bible* for the early Christians. So what does this story tell us about the way in which the earliest Christians used that Bible (now called the Old Testament by Christians)?

▶ Jesus had asked his disciples *not* to go around telling everyone that he was the Messiah. Why do you think he should now decide to make such a public demonstration of the fact that he regarded himself as a king (the Messiah)?

Son of David?

As Jesus was teaching in the Temple, he asked the question: 'How can the teachers of the Law say that the Messiah will be the descendant of David? The Holy Spirit inspired David to say:
"The Lord said to my Lord:
Sit here on my right
until I put your enemies under your feet."
David himself called him "Lord"; so how can the Messiah be David's descendant?'

(12:35–37)

Jesus' entry into Jerusalem, from the Oberammergau Passion Play

It was firmly expected that the Messiah would be a direct descendant of King David, and he would become the head of what would basically be David's kingdom – recovered and restored for ever. So, 'Son of David' was one of the ways in which people talked about the Messiah.

Psalm 110, from which this quote comes, was regarded as a prophetic song about the coming Messiah. At the time it was thought to have been composed by David, although it now seems as if it was written no more than 200 years before Jesus.

FOR DISCUSSION

▶ What point do you think Jesus is trying to make here?

19 GOD SAYS 'YES'...

...in Baptism...

The baptism of Mike Tyson

Not long afterwards Jesus came from Nazareth in the province of Galilee, and was baptized by John in the Jordan. As soon as Jesus came up out of the water, he saw heaven opening and the Spirit coming down on him like a dove. And a voice came from heaven: 'You are my own dear Son. I am pleased with you.'

At once the Spirit made him go into the desert, where he stayed forty days, being tempted by Satan. Wild animals were also there, but angels came and helped him.

(1:9–13)

...and Transfiguration...

Six days later Jesus took with him Peter, James and John, and led them up a high mountain, where they were alone. As they looked on, a change came over Jesus, and his clothes became shining white – whiter than anyone in the world could wash them. Then the three disciples saw Elijah and Moses talking with Jesus. Peter spoke up and said to Jesus: 'Teacher, how good it is that we are here! We will make three tents, one for you, one for Moses, and one for Elijah.' He and the others were so frightened that he did not know what to say.

Then a cloud appeared and covered them with its shadow, and a voice came from the cloud: 'This is my own dear Son – listen to him!' They took a quick look round but did not see anyone else; only Jesus was with them.

As they came down the mountain, Jesus ordered them: 'Don't tell anyone what you have seen, until the Son of Man has risen from death.'

(9:2–9)

QUICK QUIZ

- ▶ In which river was Jesus baptized?
- ▶ How long did Jesus stay in the desert?
- ▶ Who came and helped him there?
- ▶ At the Transfiguration, what practical thing did Peter suggest they should do?
- ▶ Where did the voice seem to come from?

These two stories both make the same claim – that the way Jesus saw things was the way God saw things, that his thoughts were God's thoughts. Putting it another way, they are saying that when Jesus says the Messiah must suffer, God says 'yes', and when Jesus says he is the Messiah, God also says 'yes'. They leave you having to answer the questions: 'Just who do I believe Jesus is?' and 'What is his relationship to God?'

The stories make use of words and ideas from the Jewish scriptures.

42   *The Hill of Transfiguration, backed by Mount Hermon*

THE WORDS

There are three direct quotations.

The first (used in both stories) comes from a psalm that would have been sung in the Temple during the coronation of a king:

> *'I will announce,' says the king, 'what the Lord has declared.*
> *He said to me:* "You are my son: today I have become your father . . ." '
>
> (Psalm 2:7)

The second (used in the first story) comes from the first verse of the first Servant Song (see unit 14):

> *'Here is my servant, whom I strengthen – the one I have chosen, with whom I am pleased . . .'*
>
> (Isaiah 42:1)

The third (used in the second story) is the promise once made by Moses that another prophet would follow him:

> *'. . . he will send you a prophet like me from among your own people, and you are to obey him.'*
>
> (Deuteronomy 18:15)

THE IDEAS

In the story of the Flood, the *dove* leaves the Ark to come down and settle on the new world as it emerges from the water (Genesis 8:8–12). In the story of the Baptism, the *dove* leaves heaven to come down and settle on Jesus, in Christian eyes the new humanity, as he emerges from the water.

Satan is the one who tests a person's faith in and commitment to God. In the story of Job, God allows Satan to test Job. Satan makes him suffer a series of 'accidents' to property, family and friends. When this does not work, he makes him suffer an extremely painful skin-disease. This does not work either and so Job's faith in God – and God's faith in

Job – is vindicated. In time, from being simply the Tempter, Satan becomes the Evil One or the Devil. This is how he is presented in unit 21.

FOR YOUR FOLDERS

► What might the 'wild animals' represent?
► Find out what the word 'angel' means. What do you think Mark means when he says 'angels came and helped him'?

The *whiteness* of Jesus' clothes was a way of emphasizing the purity of his character and personality.

Elijah and *Moses* are the twin pillars of Judaism: Elijah represents Prophecy, Moses the Law.

The *tents* would be the shelters built by the pilgrims on their way to Jerusalem for the festival of Succot. They would be reminded – as Jews are today – of how God gave them the Law at Mount Sinai.

The *cloud* was the cloud of God's presence. It had led the people from Egypt after the Exodus; it had covered Mount Sinai and Moses had gone up into it to receive the Law; and it covered the tent which housed the Law during their travels.

THINGS TO DO

► Using the background information you have been given here about the *words* and the *ideas*, and not forgetting what you have learned from the previous units, explain in your own words what the stories of
   a The Baptism; and
   b The Transfiguration
are saying about Jesus.

TEST YOURSELF!

1 'He was arrested and sentenced and led off to die, and no-one cared about his fate.' Which book does this come from?
2 In which century were the Servant Songs originally written?
3 What is special about the Servant's suffering?
4 Who is the Servant, as far as Christians are concerned?

5 Which Hebrew/Aramaic phrase is translated by the words 'Son of Man'?
6 What three meanings could there be to the phrase 'Son of Man'?
7 How many times does the phrase 'Son of Man' appear in Mark's Gospel?
8 What does Daniel 7:13 say?
9 What does Jesus say about the Son of Man and the Sabbath?
10 What does Jesus say about the Son of Man and the idea of serving and giving?
11 In which book did the phrase 'Son of Man' become a definite Messianic title?

12 What is generally reckoned to be the date of the Crucifixion?
13 For how many years after Jesus is there no actual written evidence of Christianity?
14 What were the earliest Christian preachers saying?
15 From whom did they get their ideas?
16 How many times did Jesus predict his suffering and death?
17 Where was he for the first of these?
18 What happened when Peter challenged him on whether it was really necessary to go through with it?
19 What did John say when he appeared in the desert, baptizing and preaching?
20 What did he do with those who confessed their sins?
21 How was John dressed?
22 What food did John live on?
23 What did he say about the one who was to come after him?

24 What had John the Baptist kept telling Herod?
25 How was it that the daughter of Herodias was able to ask for the head of John the Baptist?
26 Who does Mark believe John to have been?
27 Why is this important as regards Jesus?
28 What does the word 'baptism' actually mean?

29 How many disciples did Jesus send to bring the colt?
30 Where was the colt when they found it?
31 What did they say in answer to the bystanders?
32 What other occasion have you come across where Jesus appears to have made advance arrangements in Jerusalem?
33 What had Zechariah said about how the king would come to Jerusalem?
34 What did the crowds sing as Jesus rode into Jerusalem?
35 Quote a line or two from one of the hymns which Christians sing on Palm Sunday.
36 From which Jewish king was it expected that the Messiah would be descended?
37 On what grounds did Jesus question this?

38 Where had Jesus been before his baptism?
39 After his baptism, what did he see?
40 After his baptism, what did he hear?
41 After his baptism, where did he go?
42 What happened to him there?
43 What does the story of the Baptism seem to be saying about Jesus?
44 Which three disciples are mentioned in connection with the Transfiguration story?
45 What change did they see in Jesus' appearance?
46 Who did they see talking with Jesus?
47 What did the voice from the cloud say?
48 What did Jesus say to them as they came down the mountain?
49 What does the story of the Transfiguration seem to be saying about Jesus?
50 Which part of the Jewish Bible is quoted in both the Baptism and the Transfiguration stories?

Part 3
WHAT DID JESUS DO?

Exorcisms

Most of what is known about the causes and cures of disease and illness has been discovered in the last 200 years or so. 2,000 years ago people knew absolutely nothing about modern methods of medicine – and even less about mental illness!

People who were suffering from mental or emotional disorders – who today would probably be diagnosed as schizophrenic – were thought to have evil spirits (or demons) living in them.

The only way they could be cured was if someone was strong enough to control the demon and could make it leave the person's body. The word for this is 'to exorcise' and the action which brings about a cure is an 'exorcism'.

The stories in this unit and the following one show that Jesus was someone who was able to cure people in this way.

In the Capernaum Synagogue

Jesus and his disciples came to the town of Capernaum, and on the next Sabbath Jesus went to the synagogue and began to teach. The people who heard him were amazed at the way he taught, for he wasn't like the teachers of the Law; instead, he taught with authority.

Just then a man with an evil spirit in him came into the synagogue and screamed: 'What do you want with us, Jesus of Nazareth? Are you here to destroy us? I know who you are – you are God's holy messenger!'

Jesus ordered the spirit: 'Be quiet, and come out of the man!'

The evil spirit shook the man hard, gave a loud scream, and came out of him. The people were all so amazed that they started saying to one another:

The Scream, by Edvard Munch

'What is this? Is it some kind of new teaching? The man has authority to give orders to the evil spirits, and they obey him!'

And so the news about Jesus spread quickly everywhere in the province of Galilee.

(1:21–28)

'Mob' in Gerasa

Jesus and his disciples arrived on the other side of Lake Galilee, in the territory of Gerasa. As soon as Jesus got out of the boat, he was met by a man who came out of the burial caves there. This man had an evil spirit in him and lived among the tombs. Nobody could keep him chained up anymore; many times his feet and hands had been chained, but every time he broke the chains and smashed the irons on his feet. He was too strong for anyone to control him. Day and night he wandered among the tombs and through the hills, screaming and cutting himself with stones.

He was some distance away when he saw Jesus; so he ran, fell on his knees before him, and screamed in a loud voice: 'Jesus, Son of the Most High God! What do you want with me? For God's sake, I beg you, don't punish me!' (He said this because Jesus was saying: 'Evil spirit, come out of this man!')

So Jesus asked him: 'What is your name?'

The man answered: 'My name is "Mob" – there are so many of us!' And he kept begging Jesus not to send the evil spirits out of that region.

There was a large herd of pigs nearby, feeding on a hillside. So the spirits begged Jesus: 'Send us to the pigs, and let us go into them.' He let them go, and the evil spirits went out of the man and entered the pigs. The whole herd – about two thousand pigs in all – rushed down the side of the cliff into the lake and was drowned.

The men who had been taking care of the pigs ran away and spread the news in the town and among the farms. People went out to see what had happened, and when they came to Jesus, they saw the man who used to have the mob of demons in him. He was sitting there, clothed and in his right mind; and they were all afraid. Those who had seen it told the people what had happened to the man with the demons, and about the pigs.

So they asked Jesus to leave their territory.

As Jesus was getting into the boat, the man who had had the demons begged him: 'Let me go with you!'

But Jesus would not let him. Instead, he told him: 'Go back home to your family and tell them how much the Lord has done for you and how kind he has been to you.'

So the man left and went through all the Ten Towns, telling what Jesus had done for him. And all who heard it were amazed.

(5:1–20)

FOR YOUR FOLDERS

▶ How can you tell that Gerasa was mostly a non-Jewish area?

▶ Everyone present was convinced that the death of two thousand animals saved one human life. Someone might argue that the death of animals in laboratories today saves many human lives. They might also argue that since Jesus allowed the pigs to die, he would not object to what happens in the laboratories. Do you agree or disagree? Why?

▶ Why do you think Jesus did not let the man come with him?

The Epileptic Boy

When they joined the rest of the disciples, they saw a large crowd round them and some teachers of the Law arguing with them. When the people saw Jesus, they were greatly surprised, and ran to him and greeted him. Jesus asked his disciples: 'What are you arguing with them about?'

A man in the crowd answered: 'Teacher, I brought my son to you, because he has an evil spirit in him and cannot talk. Whenever the spirit attacks him, it throws him to the ground, and he foams at the mouth, grits his teeth, and becomes stiff all over. I asked your disciples to drive the spirit out, but they could not.'

Jesus said to them: 'How unbelieving you people are! How long must I stay with you? How long do I have to put up with you? Bring the boy to me!' So they brought him to Jesus.

As soon as the spirit saw Jesus, it threw the boy into a fit, so that he fell on the ground and rolled round, foaming at the mouth. 'How long has he been like this?' Jesus asked the father.

'Ever since he was a child,' he replied. 'Many times the evil spirit has tried to kill him by throwing him in the fire and into water. Have pity on us and help us, if you possibly can!'

'Yes,' said Jesus, 'if you yourself can! Everything is possible for the person who has faith.'

The father at once cried out: 'I do have faith, but not enough. Help me to have more!'

Jesus noticed that the crowd was closing in on them, so he gave a command to the evil spirit. 'Deaf and dumb spirit,' he said, 'I order you to come out of the boy and never go into him again!'

The spirit screamed, threw the boy into a bad fit, and came out. The boy looked like a corpse, and everyone said: 'He is dead!' But Jesus took the boy by the hand and helped him to rise, and he stood up.

After Jesus had gone indoors, his disciples asked him privately: 'Why couldn't we drive the spirit out?'

'Only prayer can drive this kind out,' answered Jesus, 'nothing else can.'

(9:14–29)

FOR DISCUSSION

▶ The father realized that he needed more faith. The disciples accepted that they needed to pray more. Are these in fact the same needs or are they different? What do you think – and why?

▶ Today, the boy's condition would probably be diagnosed as epilepsy. Do you think that if Jesus were living today he would still be saying: 'Only prayer can drive this kind out; nothing else can.'?

The Syro-Phoenician Woman's Daughter

Then Jesus left and went away to the territory near the city of Tyre. He went into a house and did not want anyone to know he was there, but he could not stay hidden. A woman, whose daughter had an evil spirit in her, heard about Jesus and came to him at once and fell at his feet. The woman was a Gentile, born in the region of Phoenicia in Syria. She begged Jesus to drive the demon out of her daughter. But Jesus answered: 'Let us first feed the children. It isn't right to take the children's food and throw it to the dogs.'

'Sir,' she answered, 'even the dogs under the table eat the children's left-overs!'

So Jesus said to her: 'Because of that answer, go back home, where you will find that the demon has gone out of your daughter!'

She went home and found her child lying on the bed; the demon had indeed gone out of her.

(7:24–30)

This story is remarkable for two reasons. First, it is an example (the only one in Mark's Gospel) of Jesus healing someone without actually ever meeting them. Second, it sounded initially as if Jesus was a racist in what he said to the woman. His response to her reply, however, makes it seem as though he had spoken in a fairly 'tongue in cheek' way.

FOR DISCUSSION

▶ Some experts say that stories which present Jesus in a somewhat unfavourable light are more likely to be genuine. What do you think?

Summaries

After the sun had set and evening had come, people brought to Jesus all the sick and those who had demons. All the people of the town gathered in front of the house. Jesus healed many who were sick with all kinds of diseases and drove out many demons. He would not let the demons say anything, because they knew who he was.

(1:32–34)

Jesus and his disciples went away to Lake Galilee, and a large crowd followed him. They had come from Galilee, from Judaea, from Jerusalem, from the territory of Idumea, from the territory on the east side of the Jordan, and from the region round the cities of Tyre and Sidon. All these people came to Jesus because they had heard of the things he was doing. The crowd was so large that Jesus told his disciples to get a boat ready for him, so that the people would not crush him. He had healed many people, and all those who were ill kept pushing their way to him in order to touch him. And whenever the people who had evil spirits in them saw him, they would fall down before him and scream: 'You are the Son of God!'

Jesus sternly ordered the evil spirits not to tell anyone who he was.

(3:7–12)

FOR YOUR FOLDERS

▶ Mark keeps making the point that although people generally might not have recognized Jesus for who he was, the evil spirits certainly did. Find two more examples to illustrate this from the passages in the previous unit. Why is Mark emphasizing this so much?

Making Time For Prayer

Very early the next morning, long before daylight, Jesus got up and left the house. He went out of the town to a lonely place, where he prayed. But Simon and his companions went out searching for him, and when they found him, they said: 'Everyone is looking for you.'

But Jesus answered: 'We must go on to the other villages round here. I have to preach in them also, because that is why I came.'

So he travelled all over Galilee, preaching in the synagogues and driving out demons.

(1:35–39)

FOR YOUR FOLDERS

▶ What other example(s) have you come across of Jesus praying? What evidence is there from this passage that it was important to him?

The Work of the Devil?

Then Jesus went home again. Again such a large crowd gathered that Jesus and his disciples had no time to eat. When his family heard about it they set out to take charge of him, because people were saying: 'He's gone mad!'

Some teachers of the Law who had come from Jerusalem were saying: 'He has Beelzebul in him! It is the chief of the demons who gives him the power to drive them out.'

So Jesus called them to him and spoke to them in parables: 'How can Satan drive out Satan? If a country divides itself into groups which fight each other, that country will fall apart. If a family divides itself into groups which fight each other, that family will fall apart. So if Satan's kingdom divides into groups, it cannot last, but will fall apart and come to an end.

'No-one can break into a strong man's house and take away his belongings unless he first ties up the strong man; then he can plunder his house.

'I assure you that people can be forgiven all their sins and all the evil things they may say. But whoever says evil things against the Holy Spirit will never be forgiven, because he has committed an eternal sin.' (Jesus said this because some people were saying: 'He has an evil spirit in him.')

(3:20–30)

Jesus was not the only successful exorcist. There were others who healed people this way. To the early Christians, however, Jesus was the commander-in-chief of all the forces of goodness. He was engaged in a war against the Devil and his army of demons. Jesus' death and resurrection is therefore seen as the historical moment when the decisive battle took place and resulted in the ultimate victory.

But not everyone saw it this way. At the time, Jesus' family thought he had gone mad. The religious experts from Jerusalem decided he received his powers from an extremely nasty evil spirit. Beelzebul may be a misspelling of Beelzebub which means 'Lord of the Flies'. They were virtually accusing him of being the Devil himself.

THINGS TO DO

▶ Explain in your own words what Jesus had to say in reply to the accusation that he was in league with the Devil.

▶ Verse 29 ('. . . *whoever says evil things against the Holy Spirit will never be forgiven . . .*') seems very harsh. Imagine you were alive then. What sort of things might you have said to Jesus to try to make him change his mind?

Proof Wanted

Some Pharisees came to Jesus and started to argue with him. They wanted to trap him, so they asked him to perform a miracle to show that God approved of him. But Jesus gave a deep groan and said: 'Why do the people of this day ask for a miracle? No, I tell you! No such proof will be given to these people!'

He left them, got back into the boat, and started across to the other side of the lake.

(8:11–13)

FOR DISCUSSION

▶ If Jesus had performed a miracle at the Pharisees' request, would it have proved anything?

Disciples do the same as Jesus

Then Jesus went to the villages round there, teaching the people. He called the twelve disciples together and sent them out two by two. He gave them authority over the evil spirits and ordered them: 'Don't take anything with you on your journey except a stick – no bread, no beggar's bag, no money in your pockets. Wear sandals, but don't carry an extra shirt.' He also said: 'Wherever you are welcomed, stay in the same house until you leave that place. If you come to a town where people do not welcome you or will not listen to you, leave it and shake the dust off your feet. That will be a warning to them!'

So they went out and preached that people should turn away from their sins. They drove out many demons, and rubbed olive-oil on many sick people and healed them.

(6:7–13)

THINGS TO DO

▶ Imagine that you are one of the disciples and write an account of the sorts of things that happened to you.

In this unit and unit 23 we shall be looking at the stories of how people were healed through being touched by Jesus. What comes across very strongly in these stories is a growing belief that an enormous power of healing was being physically transmitted by Jesus.

Peter's Mother-in-Law

Jesus and his disciples, including James and John, left the synagogue and went straight to the home of Simon and Andrew. Simon's mother-in-law was sick in bed with a fever, and as soon as Jesus arrived he was told about her. He went to her, took her by the hand, and helped her up. The fever left her, and she began to wait on them.

(1:29–31)

This is obviously one of the things that Peter would have remembered and then related to Mark (see unit 40).

Man with a Skin Disease

A man suffering from a dreaded skin disease came to Jesus for help. 'If you want to,' he said, 'you can make me clean.'

Jesus was filled with pity, and stretched out his hand and touched him. 'I do want to,' he answered. 'Be clean!' At once the disease left the man, and he was clean. Then Jesus spoke sternly to him and sent him away at once, after saying to him: 'Listen, don't tell anyone about this. But go straight to the priest and let him examine you; then in order to prove to everyone that you are cured, offer the sacrifice that Moses ordered.'

But the man went away and began to spread the news everywhere. Indeed, he talked so much that Jesus could not go into a town publicly. Instead, he stayed out in lonely places, and people came to him from everywhere.

(1:40–45)

The man in the story has traditionally been described as a 'leper'. But the Greek word which was translated as 'leprosy' in fact covers a whole range of skin complaints and is not necessarily just the leprosy we know today.

Woman in the Crowd

Jesus went back across to the other side of the lake. There at the lakeside a large crowd gathered round him. Jairus, an official of the local synagogue, arrived, and when he saw Jesus, he threw himself down at his feet and begged him earnestly. 'My little daughter is very ill. Please come and place your hands on her, so that she will get well and live!'

Then Jesus started off with him. So many people were going along with Jesus that they were crowding him from every side.

There was a woman who had suffered terribly from severe bleeding for twelve years, even though she had been treated by many doctors. She had spent all her money, but instead of getting better she got worse all the time. She had heard about Jesus, so she came in the crowd behind him, saying to herself: 'If I just touch his clothes, I will get well.'

She touched his cloak, and her bleeding stopped at once; and she had the feeling inside herself that she was healed of her trouble. At once Jesus knew that power had gone out of him, so he turned round in the crowd and asked: 'Who touched my clothes?'

His disciples answered: 'You see how the people are crowding you; why do you ask who touched you?'

But Jesus kept looking round to see who had done it. The woman realized what had happened to her, so she came, trembling with fear, knelt at his feet, and told him the whole truth. Jesus said to her: 'My daughter, your faith has made you well. Go in peace, and be healed of your trouble.'

(5:21–34)

Mark begins the story of the healing of Jairus' daughter but interrupts it with the story of the healing of the woman in the crowd.

Today, perhaps, a doctor might diagnose a fibroid, but according to the Torah (Leviticus 15:19–30) the woman in the crowd was ritually unclean. By touching Jesus she would have made him ritually unclean – at least until the evening and until he had washed his clothes and had a bath.

But Jesus would not have known that she was ritually unclean. The reason he kept on looking round and asking who had touched him was because he 'knew that power had gone out of him'. Once he had spoken to her and found an explanation, he was happy to go on.

THINGS TO DO

▶ Jesus said it was the woman's faith that had made her well. Go over her thoughts and her actions in your mind and then complete this sentence:

'Faith is ....'

Jairus' Daughter

While Jesus was saying this, some messengers came from Jairus' house and told him: 'Your daughter has died. Why bother the Teacher any longer?'

Jesus paid no attention to what they said, but told him: 'Don't be afraid, only believe.' Then he did not let anyone else go on with him except Peter and James and his brother John. They arrived at Jairus' house, where Jesus saw the confusion and heard all the loud crying and wailing. He went in and said to them: 'Why all this confusion? Why are you crying? The child is not dead – she is only sleeping!'

They laughed at him, so he put them all out, took the child's father and mother and his three disciples, and went into the room where the child was lying. He took her by the hand and said to her: 'Talitha, koum,' which means: 'Little girl, I tell you to get up!'

She got up at once and started walking around. (She was twelve years old.) When this happened, they were completely amazed. But Jesus gave them strict orders not to tell anyone, and he said: 'Give her something to eat.'

(5:35–43)

Everyone thought the girl was dead. Jesus said she was sleeping. Today we might describe it as a coma. His concern that she should be given something to eat makes it sound as if she might have been diabetic.

Jairus wanted Jesus to place his hands on his daughter because he believed that his healing power would be transmitted to her in this way. In the early Church, this continued to be one of the ways in which people were healed. Ananias restored Paul's lost sight (see Acts 9) and Paul himself later healed Publius' father of a fever (see Acts 28:8).

It also became:

● The means by which new Christians received the Holy Spirit (see, for example, Acts 8:14–17 and 19:5–6); and

● The method by which people were appointed to special tasks in the Church (= 'ordained') (see Acts 6:6 and 13:3).

THINGS TO DO

▶ Find out and make notes on the extent to which the Christian church(es) of today still practise the 'laying on of hands'.

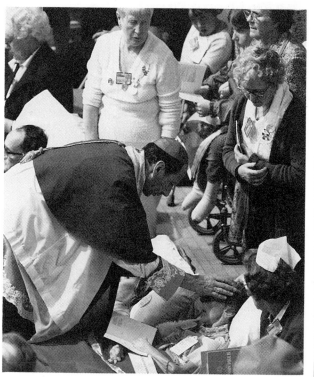

Blessing of the sick by the laying on of hands

23 CURES BY CONTACT (2)

In the first two stories in this unit Jesus does not only use physical contact. He uses his saliva to achieve a cure. This was one of the healing methods of the ancient world. The Roman historian Tacitus, for example, records that this was the method which the Emperor Vespasian used. Touching, looking towards heaven and groaning are also typical of the way that healers went about their work.

FOR YOUR FOLDERS

▶ There are two other occasions in Mark's Gospel when the actual Aramaic words are recorded. What are they?

The Blind Man at Bethsaida

They came to Bethsaida, where some people brought a blind man to Jesus and begged him to touch him. Jesus took the blind man by the hand and led him out of the village. After spitting on the man's eyes, Jesus placed his hands on him and asked him: 'Can you see anything?'

The man looked up and said: 'Yes, I can see people, but they look like trees walking about.'

Jesus again placed his hands on the man's eyes. This time the man looked intently, his eyesight returned, and he saw everything clearly. Jesus then sent him home with the order: 'Don't go back into the village.'

(8:22–26)

From the way in which the story reads, it appears that although the healing took place at Bethsaida, the man actually lived somewhere else.

Overcoming disability – deafness . . .

The Deaf and Dumb Man

Jesus then left the neighbourhood of Tyre and went through Sidon to Lake Galilee, going by way of the territory of the Ten Towns. Some people brought him a man who was deaf and could hardly speak, and they begged Jesus to place his hands on him. So Jesus took him off alone, away from the crowd, put his fingers in the man's ears, spat, and touched the man's tongue. Then Jesus looked up to heaven, gave a deep groan, and said to the man: 'Ephphatha,' which means: 'Open up!'

At once the man was able to hear, his speech impediment was removed, and he began to talk without any trouble. Then Jesus ordered the people not to speak of it to anyone; but the more he ordered them not to, the more they spoke. And all who heard were completely amazed. 'How well he does everything!' they exclaimed. 'He even causes the deaf to hear and the dumb to speak!'

(7:31–37)

Mark is probably reminded of the verse in Isaiah (35:5): *'The blind will be able to see, and the deaf will hear.'*

. . . and blindness

Summary

They crossed the lake and came to land at Gennesaret, where they tied up the boat. As they left the boat, people recognized Jesus at once. So they ran throughout the whole region; and wherever they heard he was, they brought to him sick people lying on their mats. And everywhere Jesus went, to villages, towns, or farms, people would take those who were ill to the market places and beg him to let them at least touch the edge of his cloak; and all who touched him were made well.

(6:53–56)

This 'summary statement' emphasizes not only the way in which people were healed by touching Jesus, but also the lengths to which they would go to obtain healing.

There is no doubt that, as far as they were concerned, and as far as Mark was concerned, Jesus was full of the power to heal. In unit 21, Jesus defended himself against the charge that it was black magic. But the question still remains as a sort of standing challenge: 'Where does Jesus get this power from?'

FOR YOUR FOLDERS

▶ What answer do you think Mark wants us to give?
▶ What further questions does such an answer raise?

Nazareth

Jesus left that place and went back to his home town, followed by his disciples. On the Sabbath he began to teach in the synagogue. Many people were there; and when they heard him they were all amazed. 'Where did he get all this?' they asked. 'What wisdom is this that has been given him? How does he perform miracles? Isn't he the carpenter, the son of Mary, and the brother of James, Joseph, Judas, and Simon? Aren't his sisters living here?' And so they rejected him.

Jesus said to them: 'A prophet is respected everywhere except in his own home town and by his relatives and his family.'

He was not able to perform any miracles there, except that he placed his hands on a few sick people and healed them. He was greatly surprised, because the people did not have faith.

(6:1–6)

Too much familiarity and too little faith are the reasons given for Jesus' 'failure' at Nazareth.

For more about Jesus and his family see unit 33.

FOR DISCUSSION

▶ What sort of faith do you think Jesus wanted the people to have?

QUICK QUIZ

▶ What does 'Ephphatha' mean?
▶ Who said: 'I can see people, but they look like trees walking about'?
▶ Why did those who were ill want to touch the edge of Jesus' cloak?
▶ What did Jesus say about the reception he received at Nazareth?
▶ What surprised him about the people there?

24 CURES BY CONVERSATION

In the three stories in this unit, there are no exorcisms and there is no physical contact of any sort. Jesus achieves the cures simply by talking.

The Paralyzed Man

A few days later Jesus went back to Capernaum, and the news spread that he was at home. So many people came together that there was no room left, not even out in front of the door. Jesus was preaching the message to them when four men arrived, carrying a paralyzed man to Jesus. Because of the crowd, however, they could not get the man to him. So they made a hole in the roof right above the place where Jesus was. When they had made an opening, they let the man down, lying on his mat. Seeing how much faith they had, Jesus said to the paralyzed man: 'My son, your sins are forgiven.'

Some teachers of the Law who were sitting there thought to themselves: 'How does he dare to talk like this? This is blasphemy! God is the only one who can forgive sins!'

At once Jesus knew what they were thinking, so he said to them: 'Why do you think such things? Is it easier to say to this paralyzed man, "Your sins are forgiven", or to say, "Get up, pick up your mat, and walk"? I will prove to you, then, that the Son of Man has authority on earth to forgive sins.' So he said to the paralyzed man: 'I tell you, get up, pick up your mat, and go home!'

While they all watched, the man got up, picked up his mat, and hurried away. They were all completely amazed and praised God, saying: 'We have never seen anything like this!'

(2:1–12)

The man's condition appears to have been a psychosomatic one; that is to say, his physical paralysis was probably caused by the power of his guilt feelings.

Somehow or other Jesus was aware of this, because he ignored the man's physical condition and concentrated on getting rid of his guilt by convincing him that he was forgiven. Once this had been achieved, the paralysis disappeared.

It is certainly true that in traditional Jewish thought only God could forgive sins. Jesus was trying to convince the man that his sins had been forgiven – which may or may not be the same thing!

FOR DISCUSSION

► Note that it was when Jesus saw how much faith the four men had (not the paralyzed man), that he told the man his sins were forgiven. To what extent do you think cures depend on the relatives and friends rather than on the patients themselves?

The Man with a Paralyzed Hand

Then Jesus went back to the synagogue, where there was a man who had a paralyzed hand. Some people were there who wanted to accuse Jesus of doing wrong; so they watched him closely to see whether he would heal the man on the Sabbath. Jesus said to the man: 'Come up here to the front.' Then he asked the people: 'What does our Law allow us to do on the Sabbath? To help or to harm? To save a man's life or to destroy it?'

But they did not say a thing. Jesus was angry as he looked round at them, but at the same time he felt sorry for them, because they were so stubborn and wrong. Then he said to the man; 'Stretch out your hand.' He stretched it out, and it became well again.

So the Pharisees left the synagogue and met at once with some members of Herod's party, and they made plans to kill Jesus.

(3:1–6)

The Torah says there must be no work done on the Sabbath (see Exodus 20:8–11). Most teachers of the Law said medical attention should be given on the Sabbath if a person's life was in danger. In the case of the man with the paralyzed hand, of course, the man's life was not in danger.

This story is a part of the argument which went on between Jesus and the Pharisees and the teachers of the Law about what should and should not be allowed on the Sabbath (see unit 32).

Jesus here acted in a very provocative manner and the Pharisees clearly decided that enough was enough.

THINGS TO DO

▶ Is there anything, do you think, that Jesus would not do on the Sabbath? Give reasons for your answer.

▶ There are some Christian groups (like the Seventh Day Adventists) who worship on the Sabbath (or Saturday) rather than on a Sunday. Find out why they do this.

FOR YOUR FOLDERS

▶ Why do you think the people told Bartimaeus to be quiet?

▶ Once again Jesus says it is faith that has made him able to see again. What would you say faith is in Bartimaeus' case?

Seventh Day Adventists

Bartimaeus

They came to Jericho, and as Jesus was leaving with his disciples and a large crowd, a blind beggar named Bartimaeus, son of Timaeus, was sitting by the road. When he heard that it was Jesus of Nazareth, he began to shout: 'Jesus! Son of David! Take pity on me!'

Many of the people scolded him and told him to be quiet. But he shouted even more loudly: 'Son of David, take pity on me!'

Jesus stopped and said: 'Call him.'

So they called the blind man. 'Cheer up!' they said. 'Get up, he is calling you.'

He threw off his cloak, jumped up, and came to Jesus.

'What do you want me to do for you?' Jesus asked him.

'Teacher,' the blind man answered, 'I want to see again.'

'Go,' Jesus told him, 'your faith has made you well.'

At once he was able to see and followed Jesus on the road.

(10:46–52)

Miracles

'Dunamis' – power at work

The Greek word 'dunamis', which is often translated as 'miracle', gives us English words like 'dynamo', 'dynamite' and 'dynamic'. These are all words which speak of power. A dynamo is a source of electric power; dynamite is a substance which has the power to blow up things; and dynamic is often used to describe a lively personality.

We often think of a miracle as being something quite unnatural and extraordinary – as if God totally ignores what we might call the 'laws of nature'. But this is not what the New Testament word means.

The idea which the word 'dunamis' is trying to convey is that a miracle is an occasion when God's power can be seen to be at work. 'Mighty act' is one translation that goes some way to capturing the real meaning.

Mark is not claiming that Jesus was unique in being able to cure people. What he is saying is that Jesus was so uniquely full of the power of God that he was setting people free wherever he went.

There are two stories here. The basic outline of both is so similar that most experts are convinced they are different versions of the same original.

In one, 5,000 people are fed from five loaves and two fishes and there are twelve baskets of leftovers. In the other, 4,000 people are fed from seven loaves and a few small fish and there are seven baskets of leftovers.

Modern day readers are left with a choice. They can either regard the two stories as accurate accounts of exactly what took place. Or they can regard them as so factually unbelievable that the all-important question becomes: 'What are they trying to say?'

We will divide the stories into three parts and look at each part in turn: the build-up, the story itself, and the sequel.

The Build-up

The apostles returned and met with Jesus, and told him all they had done and taught. There were so many people coming and going that Jesus and his disciples didn't even have time to eat. So he said to them: 'Let us go off by ourselves to some place where we will be alone and you can rest for a while.' So they started out in a boat by themselves for a lonely place.

Many people, however, saw them leave and knew at once who they were; so they went from all the towns and ran ahead by land and arrived at the place ahead of Jesus and his disciples. When Jesus got out of the boat, he saw this large crowd, and his heart was filled with pity for them, because they were like sheep without a shepherd. So he began to teach them many things. When it was getting late, his disciples came to him and said: 'It is already very late, and this is a lonely place. Send the people away, and let them go to the nearby farms and villages in order to buy themselves something to eat.'

'You yourselves give them something to eat,' Jesus answered.

They asked: 'Do you want us to go and spend two hundred silver coins on bread in order to feed them?'

So Jesus asked them: 'How much bread have you got? Go and see.'

When they found out, they told him: 'Five loaves and also two fish.'

(6:30–38)

Not long afterwards another large crowd came together. When the people had nothing left to eat, Jesus called the disciples to him and said: 'I feel sorry for these people, because they have been with me for three days and now have nothing to eat. If I send them home without feeding them, they will faint as they go, because some of them have come a long way.'

His disciples asked him: 'Where in this desert can anyone find enough food to feed all these people?'

'How much bread have you got?' Jesus asked.
'Seven loaves,' they answered.

(8:1–5)

The scene has been set: a huge number of people in the middle of the desert with absolutely nothing to eat. It is very similar to the story of the people of Israel who, having escaped from Egypt, complained to Moses: 'You have brought us out into this desert to starve us all to death.'

Moses promised that God would provide food for them and, sure enough, each morning the ground was covered in manna, a small white seed which tasted like biscuits made with honey.

So perhaps the story in Mark is already saying that Jesus is the new Moses – but with a difference – he provides the food *himself*.

The Story

Jesus then told his disciples to make all the people divide into groups and sit down on the green grass. So the people sat down in rows, in groups of 100 and groups of fifty. Then Jesus took the five loaves and the two fish, looked up to heaven, and gave thanks to God. He broke the loaves and gave them to his disciples to distribute to the people. He also divided the two fish among them all. Everyone ate and had enough. Then the disciples took up twelve baskets full of what was left of the bread and the fish. The number of men who were fed was 5,000.

(6:39–44)

He ordered the crowd to sit down on the ground. Then he took the seven loaves, gave thanks to God, broke them, and gave them to his disciples to distribute to the crowd; and the disciples did so. They also had a few small fish. Jesus gave thanks for these and told the disciples to distribute them too. Everybody ate and had enough – there were about 4,000 people. Then the disciples took up seven baskets full of pieces left over.

(8:6–9)

What is happening here? They are all sitting down . . . Jesus is taking the bread . . . He is giving thanks to God . . . breaking the bread . . . giving it to his disciples . . . to distribute to the people . . . . And could it be that he is saying: 'Take it, this is my body'? In other words, the desert has become the Upper Room; the manna is now the bread of the Holy Communion; and Moses has been replaced by Jesus. Thre is more than enough for everyone – and there is still plenty to spare!

QUICK QUIZ

▶ What other story have you come across in which Jesus replaces Moses?

The Sequel(s)

Jesus sent the people away and at once got into a boat with his disciples and went to the district of Dalmanutha. . . . The disciples had forgotten to bring enough bread and had only one loaf with them in the boat. 'Take care,' Jesus warned them, 'and be on your guard against the yeast of the Pharisees and the yeast of Herod.'

They started discussing among themselves: 'He says this because we haven't any bread.'

Jesus knew what they were saying, so he asked them: 'Why are you discussing about not having any bread? Don't you know or understand yet? Are your minds so dull? You have eyes – can't you see? You have ears – can't you hear? Don't you remember when I broke the five loaves for the 5,000 people? How many baskets full of leftover pieces did you take up?'

'Twelve' they answered.

'And when I broke the seven loaves for the 4,000 people,' asked Jesus, 'how many baskets full of leftover pieces did you take up?'

'Seven,' they answered.

'And you still don't understand?' he asked them.
(8:10 and 14–21)

Yeast is something which works in a 'hidden' way but which has a tremendous influence and effect. It brings about some enormous changes. Elsewhere Jesus used this idea to talk about the Kingdom of God. Here he is talking about the Pharisees and Herod. He ran into problems with the Pharisees because of their attitude to the Law and the tradition (see unit 31). Herod had completely misunderstood who Jesus was (see unit 17).

FOR YOUR FOLDERS

▶ What sort of wrong ideas could people quite easily get about the feeding of the 4,000 (or the 5,000)?

At once Jesus made his disciples get into the boat and go ahead of him to Bethsaida, on the other side of the lake, while he sent the crowd away. After saying goodbye to the people, he went away to a hill to pray. When evening came, the boat was in the middle of the lake, while Jesus was alone on land. He saw that his disciples were straining at the oars, because they were rowing against the wind, so some time between three and six o'clock in the morning he came to them, walking on the water. 'It's a ghost!' they thought, and screamed. They were all terrified when they saw him.

Jesus spoke to them at once. 'Courage!' he said. 'It is I. Don't be afraid!' Then he got into the boat with them, and the wind died down. The disciples were completely amazed, because they had not understood the real meaning of the feeding of the five thousand; their minds could not grasp it.
(6:45–52)

This story is like a resurrection story. Jesus appears when they are least expecting him; they do not recognize him immediately; they think he is a ghost; and their reaction is one of terror. He has to convince them that it is in fact him.

The first creation story in Genesis (1:1–3) begins:

'In the beginning, when God created the universe, the earth was formless and desolate. The raging ocean that covered everything was engulfed in total darkness, and the power of God was moving over the water . . .'

In Mark's story, Jesus comes to them walking on (moving over?) the water.

FOR YOUR FOLDERS

▶ Given this background information, what do you think was 'the real meaning of the feeding of the 5,000' (6:52)?

Storm on the Lake

On the evening of that same day Jesus said to his disciples: 'Let us go across to the other side of the lake.' So they left the crowd; the disciples got into the boat in which Jesus was already sitting, and they took him with them. Other boats were there too. Suddenly a strong wind blew up, and the waves began to spill over into the boat, so that it was about to fill with water. Jesus was in the back of the boat, sleeping with his head on a pillow. The disciples woke him up and said: 'Teacher, don't you care that we are about to die?'

Jesus stood up and commanded the wind: 'Be quiet!' and he said to the waves: 'Be still!' The wind died down, and there was a great calm. Then Jesus said to his disciples: 'Why are you frightened? Have you still no faith?'

But they were terribly afraid and said to one another: 'Who is this man? Even the wind and the waves obey him!'

(4:35–41)

Sudden storms are one of the hazards of Lake Galilee which is only about five miles across. In those days, they would have been regarded as the work of evil spirits. For Mark, therefore, the story shows how much power Jesus had: 'Even the wind and the waves obey him.'

Some experts, however, say that although that is how the story presents things *now*, it may not be what actually happened in the first place.

Read the story again, and this time take out the words: 'the wind' and 'the waves'. The effect is that that particular sentence now reads: 'Jesus stood up and commanded: "Be quiet! . . . Be still!"' Who was he speaking to? Presumably to the disciples. The fact that the storm died down at that point made them think that he was speaking to the evil spirits in the environment, not to them.

FOR YOUR FOLDERS

▶ How important is it that Jesus should be seen as being able to control the natural environment – things like wind and water or, come to that, earth and fire as well? Would it make him any less a person than he is claimed to be if he were *not* able to? Give reasons for your answers.

The Fig Tree

The next day, as they were coming back from Bethany, Jesus was hungry. He saw in the distance a fig tree covered with leaves, so he went to see if he could find any figs on it. But when he came to it, he found only leaves, because it was not the right time for figs. Jesus said to the fig tree: 'No-one shall ever eat figs from you again!'

And his disciples heard him . . . .

Early next morning, as they walked along the road, they saw the fig tree. It was dead all the way down to its roots. Peter remembered what had happened and said to Jesus: 'Look, Teacher, the fig tree you cursed has died!'

(11:12–14 and 20–21)

Fishing on the Sea of Galilee

Fig trees usually come into leaf by the end of March or beginning of April. The main fruit crop is not until August. At around Passover time (March–April), there are often some very small figs, known as the 'winter-crop', which are not really worth eating. Their presence would, however, give some reassurance that the tree was likely to bear fruit in the summer. If there were none there at all, it could mean there would be no main crop later.

In Matthew's Gospel, completed after Mark's, the story has changed:

On his way back to the city early next morning, Jesus was hungry. He saw a fig tree by the side of the road and went to it, but found nothing on it except leaves. So he said to the tree: 'You will never again bear fruit!' At once the fig tree dried up.

The disciples saw this and were astounded. 'How did the fig tree dry up so quickly?' they asked.

(Matthew 21:18–20)

In Luke's Gospel, completed at around the same time as Matthew's, Jesus tells a parable about a fig tree.

'There was once a man who had a fig tree growing in his vineyard. He went looking for figs on it but found none. So he said to his gardener: "Look, for three years I have been coming here looking for figs on this fig tree, and I haven't found any. Cut it down! Why should it go on using up the soil?" But the gardener answered: "Leave it alone, sir, just one more year; I will dig round it and put in some manure. Then if the tree bears figs next year, so much the better; if not, then you can have it cut down."'

(Luke 13:6–9)

FOR DISCUSSION

▶ What do you make of it all? Did Jesus actually put a curse on the fig tree? Or is that not a little out of character? Did the fig tree dry up immediately? Or did it happen overnight? Did the incident develop into the parable? Or did the parable develop into the incident as it is in Mark and then maybe as it is in Matthew? Or do you have any other thoughts or ideas?

Real Faith

Jesus goes on to talk about the need to believe that what you are praying for will really happen.

Jesus answered them: 'Have faith in God, I assure you that whoever tells this hill to get up and throw itself in the sea and does not doubt in his heart, but believes that what he says will happen, it will be done for him. For this reason I tell you: When you pray and ask for something, believe that you have received it, and you will be given whatever you ask for. And when you stand and pray, forgive anything you may have against anyone, so that your Father in heaven will forgive the wrongs you have done.'

(11:22–25)

FOR YOUR FOLDERS

▶ 'When you pray and ask for something, believe that you have received it, and you will be given whatever you ask for.'
Do you think that Jesus may have been misquoted here? Why? Why not?

Some copyists include another verse here, which is a straight lift from Matthew's Gospel. Maybe they thought that Mark must have left it out by mistake!

If you do not forgive others, your Father in heaven will not forgive the wrongs you have done.

(11:26)

QUICK QUIZ

▶ What did the disciples say when they woke Jesus up in the middle of the storm?
▶ What did Jesus say?
▶ What happened?
▶ What did Jesus discover when he came to the fig tree?
▶ What did he say?
▶ What happened?

TEST YOURSELF!

1. In the synagogue at Capernaum, what did the man scream out at Jesus?
2. What did Jesus say to the evil spirit?
3. What did the people say about it all?
4. In which territory did 'Mob' live?
5. Whereabouts in that territory did he live?
6. Why was he called 'Mob'?
7. How many pigs were drowned?
8. For how long had the boy been epileptic?
9. How did the father reply when Jesus said: 'Everything is possible for the person who has faith.'?
10. How did Jesus answer the disciples when they asked him: 'Why couldn't we drive the spirit out?'?

11. Where did Jesus meet the Syro-Phoenician woman?
12. What was it that made Jesus drive the demon out of her daughter?
13. What is it that makes this healing unique among the healings in Mark's Gospel?
14. Why did Jesus not let the demons say anything?
15. Why did Jesus get up very early, long before daylight, and leave the house?
16. How did the teachers of the Law from Jerusalem explain the fact that Jesus was able to effect these cures?
17. How did Jesus reply to their charge?
18. Who did Jesus say could never be forgiven?
19. Why did the Pharisees ask Jesus to perform a miracle for them?
20. When Jesus sent the disciples out in pairs, what did they do to heal people?

21. How do we know that Simon Peter was married?
22. What did the man with the skin disease say to Jesus?
23. What did Jesus tell him to do, after he had cured him?
24. What position did Jairus hold in the community?
25. Why did Jesus ask who had touched his clothes?
26. What did he say to the woman who admitted that she had deliberately touched him?
27. Why did Jesus say to Jairus: 'Don't be afraid, only believe.'?
28. What did Jesus say to Jairus' daughter?

29. What did Jesus do and what did he say in order to cure the man who was deaf and could hardly speak?
30. What was the reaction of those who heard about it?
31. Where did this take place?
32. How did Jesus restore the sight of the blind man at Bethsaida?
33. What evidence is there in Mark's Gospel of Jesus' tremendous popularity?
34. Why did Jesus 'fail' at Nazareth?

35. What did Jesus say to the paralyzed man?
36. What did the teachers of the Law think to themselves when he said this?
37. How did Jesus prove that the man's sins were forgiven?
38. What did the Pharisees do when Jesus healed the man with the paralyzed hand in the synagogue one Sabbath?
39. What was Bartimaeus shouting to Jesus at Jericho?
40. Why was he shouting?

41. In what sort of area did the feeding of the 4,000 take place?
42. When there were seven loaves, a few small fish and seven baskets of leftovers, how many people were there?
43. When there were five loaves, two small fishes and twelve baskets of leftovers, how many people were there?
44. What happened after the feeding of the 5,000?
45. Why did the disciples think Jesus was talking about yeast after the feeding of the 4,000?

46. What did the disciples say when the storm on Lake Galilee suddenly stopped after Jesus had said: 'Be quiet!' and 'Be still!'?
47. What did Jesus say to the fig tree one day?
48. What had happened to it by the next day?
49. What sort of attitude did Jesus say his followers should have towards God when they said their prayers?
50. What sort of attitude did Jesus say his followers should have towards other people when they said their prayers?

Part 4
WHAT DID JESUS SAY?

The Phrase in Mark

The phrase 'Kingdom of God' (or 'Kingdom of heaven' as it is in Matthew) seems to be a favourite one with Jesus – certainly as far as Matthew, Mark and Luke are concerned anyway. Like 'Son of Man', it tends not to appear elsewhere in the letters or literature of the Christian New Testament.

You have come across it on two occasions already:

● At the last meal with his disciples, Jesus said he would not drink wine again until he drank the new wine in the Kingdom of God (unit 5).
● Joseph of Arimathea, who buried the body of Jesus, is described as someone 'who was waiting for the coming of the Kingdom of God' (unit 12).

The occasions you have not yet come across are when Jesus said:

● That there were some present who would not die until they had seen the Kingdom of God come with power (unit 33).
● That child-like qualities were needed to receive the Kingdom of God (unit 29).
● That it was hard for rich people to enter the Kingdom of God (unit 29).
● That people should try to get rid of whatever was stopping them entering the Kingdom of God (unit 30).
● That to regard love to God and love to one's neighbour as far more important than the ritual of religion is to be 'not far from the Kingdom of God' (unit 36).

The other occasions when the phrase appears in Mark are in the passages quoted in this unit.

The Kingdom of God is Near

After John had been put in prison, Jesus went to Galilee and preached the Good News from God. 'The right time has come,' he said, 'and the Kingdom of God is near! Turn away from your sins and believe the Good News!'

(1:14–15)

The 'Kingdom of God' is an idea which we may find difficult to understand. It is certainly not like the United Kingdom with its constitutional monarchy. The closest would be a republic with a president but no parliament.

The 'Kingdom of God' is obviously where God reigns. But he might not be recognized as king by people who are in a state of rebellion and who refuse to accept his kingship. To be king 'by right' is one thing; to be king 'in fact' is another. For this reason Christians would say that, in one sense, the kingdom of God is the whole world; in another, it is only among those who accept and obey his rule.

This also explains why, in the examples you have come across so far, the 'Kingdom of God' is mostly thought of as something which is still coming and not as something which has already arrived.

Parables about the Kingdom of God

When Jesus was alone, some of those who had heard him came to him with the twelve disciples and asked him to explain the parables. 'You have been given the secret of the Kingdom of God,' Jesus answered. 'But the others, who are on the outside, hear all things by means of parables, so that,
*   "They may look and look,*
*   yet not see;*
*   they may listen and listen,*
*   yet not understand.*
*   For if they did, they would turn to God,*
*   and he would forgive them." '*

(4:10–12)

Jesus went on to say: 'The Kingdom of God is like this. A man scatters seed in his field. He sleeps at night, is up and about during the day, and all the while the seeds are sprouting and growing. Yet he does not know how it happens. The soil itself makes the plants grow and bear fruit; first the tender stalk appears, then the ear, and finally the ear full of corn. When the corn is ripe, the man starts cutting it with his sickle, because harvest time has come.

'What shall we say the Kingdom of God is like?' asked Jesus. 'What parable shall we use to explain it? It is like this. A man takes a mustard seed, the smallest seed in the world, and plants it in the ground. After a while it grows up and becomes the biggest of all plants. It puts out such large branches

'. . . harvest time has come . . .'

that the birds come and make their nests in its shade.'

Jesus preached his message to the people, using many other parables like these; he told them as much as they could understand. He would not speak to them without using parables, but when he was alone with his disciples, he would explain everything to them.

(4:26–34)

What is a Parable?

The word 'parable' has two meanings:

- It means 'putting beside', that is, 'comparing'. For Jesus, it meant using everyday things which were very well known to describe something which was more or less unknown.
- It means a 'riddle', something which some people are able to solve but which to others remains a mystery.

FOR YOUR FOLDERS

▶ Which of the two meanings of the word 'parable' is being used in the above extracts:
  a 4:10–12?
  b 4:26–34?

▶ Which of the following phrases do you think best completes this sentence, as far as the first of the two parables is concerned? Explain why you chose that particular phrase.
  'The Kingdom of God is something . . .
    . . . which happens purely by chance.'
    . . . which grows without anyone noticing.'
    . . . which is planned from start to finish.'

▶ Now do the same thing for the second of the two parables, but this time with these phrases:
  'The Kingdom of God is something . . .
    . . . which will one day rule the whole world.'
    . . . which some people get out of all proportion to its importance.'
    . . . which grows to an enormous size from hardly anything.'

The Allegory (Parable) of the Sower

Again Jesus began to teach beside Lake Galilee. The crowd that gathered round him was so large that he got into a boat and sat in it. The boat was out in the water, and the crowd stood on the shore at the water's edge. He used parables to teach them many things, saying to them:

'Listen! Once there was a man who went out to sow corn. As he scattered the seed in the field, some of it fell along the path, and the birds came and ate it up. Some of it fell on rocky ground, where there was little soil. The seeds soon sprouted, because the soil wasn't deep. Then, when the sun came up, it burnt the young plants; and because the roots had not grown deep enough, the plants soon dried up. Some of the seed fell among thorn bushes, which grew up and choked the plants, and they didn't produce any corn. But some seeds fell in good soil, and the plants sprouted, grew, and produced corn: some had thirty grains, others sixty, and others 100.'

And Jesus concluded: 'Listen, then, if you have ears!'

(4:1–9)

FOR DISCUSSION

▶ Which of the following statements do you think best expresses what the story is trying to say? Why?

● Farming can be a very hard life.
● The more widely you scatter the seed, the more likely you are to get results.
● Preparing the ground well is the first and most important step towards getting a good harvest.

In the earliest years of Christianity, many of the parables which Jesus told were turned into allegories.

An allegory is a story in which everything stands for something. Once the symbols are explained, one can begin to understand what the story is trying to say.

This has not happened in the case of the two parables in unit 27. But it has happened in the case of the parable in this unit. It has become an allegory.

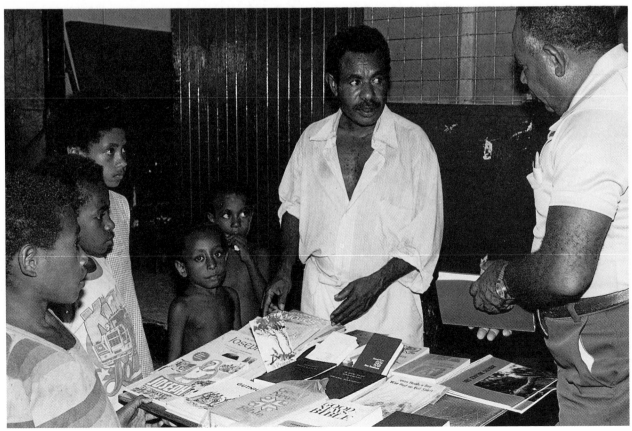

FOR YOUR FOLDERS

▶ Before you read the explanation, make a note of what *you* think the *seed* and the four types of *ground* stand for.

FOR YOUR FOLDERS

▶ Have a look at what you wrote before you read the explanation. Do you have the same as Mark?

▶ Do you think Mark is right in saying that the people are like 'the seeds'? If you were editing the original Gospel, what changes, if any, would you suggest to him?

▶ 'Listen, then, if you have ears!' . . . 'Pay attention to what you hear!' Why do you think Jesus was so anxious to get this message across?

The explanation which Mark gives is as follows:

Then Jesus asked them: 'Don't you understand this parable? How, then, will you ever understand any parable? The sower sows God's message. Some people are like the seeds that fall along the path; as soon as they hear the message, Satan comes and takes it away. Other people are like the seeds that fall on rocky ground. As soon as they hear the message, they receive it gladly. But it does not sink deep into them, and they don't last long. So when trouble or persecution comes because of the message, they give up at once. Other people are like the seeds sown among the thorn bushes. These are the ones who hear the message, but the worries about this life, the love for riches, and all other kinds of desires crowd in and choke the message, and they don't bear fruit. But other people are like the seeds sown in good soil. They hear the message, accept it, and bear fruit: some thirty, some sixty, and some 100.'

Jesus continued: 'Does anyone ever bring in a lamp and put it under a bowl or under the bed? Doesn't he put it on the lampstand? Whatever is hidden away will be brought out into the open, and whatever is covered up will be uncovered. Listen, then, if you have ears!'

He also said to them: 'Pay attention to what you hear! The same rules you use to judge others will be used by God to judge you – but with even greater severity. The person who has something will be given more, and the person who has nothing will have taken away from him even the little that he has.'

(4:13–25)

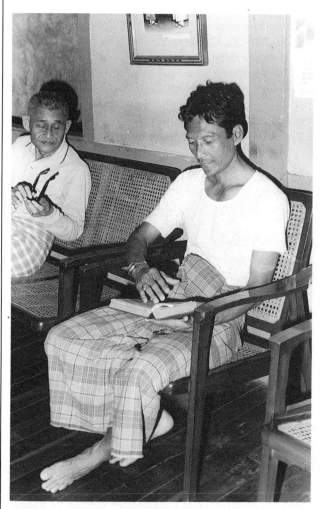

Reading the bible in Rangoon

QUICK QUIZ

▶ What happened to the seeds which
  ● fell along the path?
  ● fell on rocky ground?
  ● fell among thorn bushes?
  ● fell in good soil?
▶ What sort of people do these stand for?

First Followers

As Jesus walked along the shore of Lake Galilee, he saw two fishermen, Simon and his brother Andrew, catching fish with a net. Jesus said to them: 'Come with me, and I will teach you to catch men.' At once they left their nets and went with him.

He went a little farther on and saw two other brothers, James and John, the sons of Zebedee. They were in their boat getting their nets ready. As soon as Jesus saw them, he called them; they left their father Zebedee in the boat with the hired men and went with Jesus.

(1:16–20)

Then Jesus went up a hill and called to himself the men he wanted. They came to him, and he chose twelve, whom he named apostles. 'I have chosen you to be with me,' he told them. 'I will also send you out to preach, and you will have authority to drive out demons.'

These are the twelve he chose: Simon (Jesus gave him the name Peter); James and his brother John, the sons of Zebedee (Jesus gave them the name Boanerges, which means 'Men of Thunder'); Andrew, Philip, Bartholomew, Matthew, Thomas, James, son of Alphaeus, Thaddaeus, Simon the Patriot, and Judas Iscariot, who betrayed Jesus.

(3:13–19)

Trawling in the North Sea

'Disciple' comes from a Latin word and means a 'learner' and, in that sense, a follower. 'Apostle' also comes from a Latin word and means 'someone who is sent', in this case by Jesus.

Note that Jesus' first followers were highly skilled men who had been at the heart of the main industry centred around Lake Galilee.

Right Attitudes

They came to Capernaum, and after going indoors Jesus asked his disciples: 'What were you arguing about on the road?'

But they would not answer him, because on the road they had been arguing among themselves about who was the greatest. Jesus sat down, called the twelve disciples, and said to them: 'Whoever wants to be first must place himself last of all and be the servant of all.' Then he took a child and made him stand in front of them. He put his arms round him and said to them: 'Whoever welcomes in my name one of these children, welcomes me; and whoever welcomes me, welcomes not only me but also the one who sent me.'

(9:33–37)

Some people brought children to Jesus for him to place his hands on them, but the disciples scolded the people. When Jesus noticed this, he was angry and said to his disciples: 'Let the children come to me, and do not stop them, because the Kingdom of God belongs to such as these. I assure you that whoever does not receive the Kingdom of God like a child will never enter it.' Then he took the children in his arms, placed his hands on each of them, and blessed them.

As Jesus was starting on his way again, a man ran up, knelt before him and asked him: 'Good Teacher, what must I do to receive eternal life?'

'Why do you call me good?' Jesus asked him. 'No-one is good except God alone. You know the commandments: "Do not commit murder; do not commit adultery; do not steal; do not accuse anyone falsely; do not cheat; respect your father and your mother."'

'Teacher,' the man said, 'ever since I was young, I have obeyed all these commandments.'

Jesus looked straight at him with love and said: 'You need only one thing. Go and sell all you have and give the money to the poor, and you will have riches in heaven; then come and follow me.' When the man heard this, gloom spread over his face, and he went away sad, because he was very rich.

Jesus looked round at his disciples and said to them: 'How hard it will be for rich people to enter the Kingdom of God!'

The disciples were shocked at these words, but Jesus went on to say: 'My children, how hard it is to enter the Kingdom of God! It is much harder for a rich person to enter the Kingdom of God than for a camel to go through the eye of a needle.'

At this the disciples were completely amazed and asked one another: 'Who, then, can be saved?'

Jesus looked straight at them and answered: 'This is impossible for man, but not for God; everything is possible for God.'

Then Peter spoke up: 'Look, we have left everything and followed you.'

'Yes,' Jesus said to them, 'and I tell you that anyone who leaves home or brothers or sisters or mother or father or children or fields for me and for the Gospel, will receive much more in this present age. He will receive a hundred times more houses, brothers, sisters, mothers, children and fields – and persecutions as well; and in the age to come he will receive eternal life. But many who now are first will be last, and many who now are last will be first.'

(10:13–31)

FOR YOUR FOLDERS

▶ Here are two statements. Both try to sum up what Jesus is saying. Which one do you think is the more accurate?
  ● 'What he wants is childish people who are prepared to throw away everything they ever had to become skivvies or dog's-bodies to all and sundry.'
  ● 'What he wants is child-like people who are willing to give up the things which are precious to them for the sake of helping other people.'
Give reasons for your answer.

FOR DISCUSSION

▶ Many people regard things like health, wealth, having children and being very wise or clever as signs of God's blessing. What do you think about this?

Eternal Life

'Eternal life' (literally: 'life of the age') is a technical phrase.

Many Jews in Jesus' day believed that the age they were living in would shortly come to an end. The start of the new age would be marked by the coming of the Messiah. All the people who had ever lived would be raised from death. The quality of the lives they had lived would be assessed to see whether they were fit to live in the new age.

So 'eternal life' means (the) life of the age (to come)'. It was a life that would be lived in this world. Those who trusted Jesus and became his followers believed they were already living the life of the age to come. In this sense they were 'saved' from the judgement which they were expecting to come at the end of the present age.

It did not matter if they died before the coming of the new age. They would simply wait to be raised from death at the end of the age.

Christian thought has changed and developed over the centuries. Today, 'eternal life' is seen mostly as being 'life after death' – a life which begins in the here and now but which goes on into unending time.

There is therefore some difference between what the phrase 'eternal life' means when it is used in general conversation today and what it actually means in Mark's Gospel.

FOR YOUR FOLDERS

▶ What do you think Jesus meant by the phrase 'riches in heaven'?
▶ Without looking back at unit 27 but simply by reading through this unit very carefully, what answer would you give to the question: 'What is the Kingdom of God?'
▶ Was it simply because rich people were rich that it was hard for them to enter the Kingdom of God? Or was it something else?
▶ Why do you think 'wives' are missing from the list of people in what Jesus says to Peter?
▶ '. . . everything is possible for God.' But maybe God draws the line somewhere? What do you think? Give reasons for your answers.

About Rewards

Then James and John, the sons of Zebedee, came to Jesus. 'Teacher,' they said, 'there is something we want you to do for us.'

'What is it?' Jesus asked them.

They answered: 'When you sit on your throne in your glorious Kingdom, we want you to let us sit with you, one at your right and one at your left.'

Jesus said to them: 'You don't know what you are asking for. Can you drink the cup of suffering that I must drink? Can you be baptized in the way I must be baptized?'

'We can,' they answered.

Jesus said to them: 'You will indeed drink the cup I must drink and be baptized in the way I must be baptized. But I do not have the right to choose who will sit at my right and my left. It is God who will give these places to those for whom he has prepared them.'

When the other ten disciples heard about it, they became angry with James and John. So Jesus called them all together to him and said: 'You know that the men who are considered rulers of the heathen have power over them, and the leaders have complete authority. This, however, is not the way it is among you. If one of you wants to be great, he must be the servant of the rest; and if one of you wants to be first, he must be the slave of all. For the Son of Man did not come to be served; he came to serve and to give his life to redeem many people.'

(10:35–45)

The 'cup' and the 'baptism' of which Jesus talks are obviously ways of talking about his death. We have already come across him speaking of it as being a 'cup' (see unit 6). In unit 17 we saw how baptism for Baptists is a symbol first of dying and then starting a new life as a Christian.

James was executed by Herod Agrippa the First less than fifteen years after the death of Jesus (see Acts 12:2). His brother John apparently settled in Ephesus (now in Turkey) and eventually died peacefully as a very old man.

The word 'redeem' is best understood in the context of the pawnbroker's business. Pawnbrokers lend money to people who leave with them something of value as a 'pledge'. When they repay the money, plus the interest for the loan, the people are able to 'redeem' (or 'set free') what they have pledged. In Jesus' day, the word was used in connection with buying freedom for someone who was a slave, but basically it is the same idea.

About Competition

John said to him: 'Teacher, we saw a man who was driving out demons in your name, and we told him to stop, because he doesn't belong to our group.'

'Do not try to stop him,' Jesus told them, 'because no-one who performs a miracle in my name will be able soon afterwards to say evil things about me. For whoever is not against us is for us. I assure you that whoever gives you a drink of water because you belong to me will certainly receive his reward.'

(9:38–41)

The technical term for driving out evil spirits or demons is 'exorcism' (see unit 20).

There is a story in the Acts of the Apostles about some exorcists. In fact, they were the sons of a Jewish High Priest named Sceva. They were saying to the evil spirits: 'I command you in the name of Jesus, whom Paul preaches . . .' On this particular occasion, the evil spirit said to them: 'I know Jesus, and I know about Paul; but you – who are you?' The man then attacked them and wounded them, and they ran away with their clothes torn off.

You can read more about Jesus as an exorcist in units 20 and 21.

About Spiritual Readiness

'If anyone should cause one of these little ones to lose his faith in me, it would be better for that person to have a large millstone tied round his neck and be thrown into the sea. So if your hand makes you lose your faith, cut it off! It is better for you to enter life without a hand than to keep both hands and go off to hell, to the fire that never goes out. And if your foot makes you lose your faith, cut it off! It is better for you to enter life without a foot than to keep both feet and be thrown into hell. And if your eye makes you lose your faith, take it out! It is better for you to enter the Kingdom of God with only one eye than to keep both eyes and be thrown into hell. There "the worms that eat them never die, and the fire that burns them is never put out".

'Everyone will be purified by fire as a sacrifice is purified by salt.

'Salt is good; but if it loses its saltness, how can you make it salty again?

'Have the salt of friendship among yourselves, and live in peace with one another.'

(9:42–50)

The phrase 'these little ones' probably refers to those who are just beginning in Christianity rather than children as such.

Much of this extract reads like the script of a horror movie and, like many of them, it is probably best not to take it too literally!

The word which is translated 'hell' is 'Ge-hinnom' (valley of Hinnom). This was a valley just to the

south of Jerusalem and was the place where all the city's waste was dumped and burned. Smoke rose from it constantly and the smell was not at all inviting. It had been used in this way for centuries, and before that, so it was said, child-sacrifices had taken place there. It became a symbol for what would happen to those who were not considered fit to live in the new age when it came.

Note that Ge-hinnom was not where the dead went. In Jewish thinking they went to She-ol, a place of separation deep in the earth. They remained there 'asleep' until the general resurrection at the end of the age. She-ol was not a place of torture or torment.

The last few separate sentences are most probably individual sayings of Jesus which have been linked together by the connection first with 'fire' and then with 'salt'.

FOR YOUR FOLDERS

▶ The heading given to this extract is 'spiritual readiness'. What sort of things do you think Jesus would say people of today might have to 'cut out' of their lives in order to be more spiritually prepared?

About Selfless Giving

As Jesus sat near the Temple treasury, he watched the people as they dropped in their money. Many rich men dropped in a lot of money; then a poor widow came along and dropped in two little copper coins, worth about a penny. He called his disciples together and said to them: 'I tell you that this poor widow put more in the offering box than all of the others. For the others put in what they had to spare of their riches; but she, poor as she is, put in all she had – she gave all she had to live on.'

(12:41–44)

THINGS TO DO

▶ Imagine that you could introduce this widow to the rich man in unit 29. Write down the conversation that might take place between the two of them.

Ge-hinnom?

31 TO THE PHARISEES (1)

Background

The Pharisees were a Jewish religious movement with a very progressive outlook. They were highly respected, both for themselves and for what they sought to achieve.

Their aim was for their own lives, the lives of people in general and the life of the nation as a whole to become the sort of life required by the Torah which God had given to them through Moses. They were always striving to achieve the highest possible moral standard in everything they did.

As long as the Romans did not prevent this, the Pharisees were prepared to tolerate them, and to that extent they were not politically active.

The Pharisees were basically very open-minded towards any changes in religious ideas and practices, provided there was no conflict with the basic principles of the Torah which God had established.

For them, the divinely inspired prophets and teachers of the past and the present had been and were still seeking to guide people into the right way of life represented by the Torah.

They were prepared to accept that the spirit of a law might be more important than its letter and that God's truth was just as able to come through reasoned thinking as it was through intelligent reading. But while practices might change, the underlying principles – God's principles – must always remain the same. Jesus was bringing a new interpretation of the Torah to his generation, just as the prophets and teachers of the past had done. The Pharisees would be more than willing to listen to what he had to say – they were, after all, open to the possibility of change.

There was in fact a great deal of common ground between them, but that did not mean that the Pharisees were going to accept everything Jesus said without challenging it, questioning it and really thinking it through – and that was where the arguments came in.

Other parts of the New Testament reflect the intense bitterness and acrimony which later developed between the two camps. In reading Mark's Gospel, we certainly get some flavour of the debates between Jesus and the Pharisees.

Many of Jesus' followers started out as Pharisees. Perhaps the most famous is Paul. He studied under Gamaliel, one of the leading teachers of the Law of his day. But he was converted to Jesus' way of looking at things. He became one of the most active of all the early Church's missionaries and leaders. Before his conversion, however, Paul had, in his own words, 'savagely persecuted' the early Christians. And it was that same movement, of which Paul was part, which not only rejected the particular challenge to change which Jesus brought but also engineered his death.

Eating with Outcasts

Jesus went back again to the shore of Lake Galilee. A crowd came to him, and he started teaching them. As he walked along, he saw a tax-collector, Levi son of Alphaeus, sitting in his office. Jesus said to him: 'Follow me.' Levi got up and followed him.

Later on Jesus was having a meal in Levi's house. A large number of tax collectors and other outcasts were following Jesus, and many of them joined him and his disciples at the table. Some teachers of the Law, who were Pharisees, saw that Jesus was eating with these outcasts and tax collectors, so they asked his disciples: 'Why does he eat with such people?'

Jesus heard them and answered: 'People who are well do not need a doctor, but only those who are sick. I have not come to call respectable people, but outcasts.'

(2:13–17)

In order to get the taxes collected, the Romans offered franchises. The person who had the franchise would then charge more than the actual amount of tax and keep the difference. Many tax collectors became rich and most were hated by the ordinary people, for obvious reasons.

Levi left tax collecting and became known as Matthew. He was probably the author of a great deal of the material in the first Gospel, which is named after him.

'Other outcasts' would be a variety of people who for one reason or another were ritually unclean as far as their religion was concerned.

Jesus made it quite clear where he felt his particular mission lay – with those with whom most of the other religious teachers would have nothing to do.

THINGS TO DO

▶ The Salvation Army is a modern-day Christian organization that spends a great deal of its time seeking to serve those in need in our society. Find out more about what it does and why it does it.

Ritual Washing

Some Pharisees and teachers of the Law who had come from Jerusalem gathered round Jesus. They noticed that some of his disciples were eating their food with hands that were ritually unclean – that is, they had not washed them in the way the Pharisees said people should.

(For the Pharisees, as well as the rest of the Jews, follow the teaching they received from their ancestors; they do not eat unless they wash their hands in the proper way; nor do they eat anything that comes from the market unless they wash it first. And they follow many other rules which they have received, such as the proper way to wash cups, pots, copper bowls, and beds.)

So the Pharisees and the teachers of the Law asked Jesus: 'Why is it that your disciples do not follow the teaching handed down by our ancestors, but instead eat with ritually unclean hands?'

Jesus answered them: 'How right Isaiah was when he prophesied about you! You are hypocrites, just as he wrote:

"These people, says God, honour me with their words,
but their heart is really far away from me.
It is no use for them to worship me, because they teach manmade rules
as though they were God's laws!"
'You put aside God's command and obey the teachings of men.'

And Jesus continued: 'You have a clever way of rejecting God's law in order to uphold your own teaching. For Moses commanded: "Respect your father and your mother," and "Whoever curses his father or his mother is to be put to death". But you teach that if a person has something he could use to help his father or mother, but says "This is corban" (which means it belongs to God), he is excused from helping his father or mother. In this way the teaching you pass on to others cancels out the word of God. And there are many other things like this that you do.'

(7:1–13)

The way in which Jesus used this quote from Isaiah shows something of the intensity of the feelings that were being generated.

A 'hypocrite' is someone who pretends to be something other than what he/she really is. In the Greek theatre it referred to the mask which an actor would hold in front of his face when playing a part.

Jesus promptly changed the subject to a practice which he felt was capable of standing in the way of the spirit of the particular commandment and which therefore should be put right. It would have been interesting to have known the Pharisees' response.

Respecting the Sabbath

Jesus was walking through some cornfields on the Sabbath. As his disciples walked along with him, they began to pick the ears of corn. So the Pharisees said to Jesus: 'Look, it is against our Law for your disciples to do that on the Sabbath!'

Jesus answered: 'Have you never read what David did that time when he needed something to eat? He and his men were hungry, so he went into the house of God and ate the bread offered to God. This happened when Abiathar was the High Priest. According to our Law, only the priests may eat this bread – but David ate it and even gave it to his men.'

And Jesus concluded: 'The Sabbath was made for the good of man; man was not made for the Sabbath. So the Son of Man is lord even of the Sabbath.'

(2:23–28)

The Torah says (in Exodus 20:8–10 and Deuteronomy 5:12–14):

'Observe the Sabbath and keep it holy. You have six days in which to do your work, but the seventh day is a day of rest dedicated to me. On that day no-one is to work . . .'

But what exactly did 'work' mean? The Pharisees said that rubbing ears of corn together in one's hands to remove the husks was 'threshing' and therefore work. And they would argue: 'If you don't draw the line somewhere, there will be no weekly day off at all.'

If you read the story about David and his men in 1 Samuel 21:1–6, you will find that he does not steal the bread – which is what you might have thought from what Mark says!

THINGS TO DO

▶ Make a list of all the arguments you can think of for and against shops being open on Sundays. You may be able to talk to some local shopkeepers, local politicians, representatives of local religious groups and other local people about it.
▶ What is your own opinion?

Open all day, every day

Question of Divorce

Then Jesus left that place, went to the province of Judaea, and crossed the river Jordan. Crowds came flocking to him again, and he taught them, as he always did.

Some Pharisees came to him and tried to trap him. 'Tell us,' they asked, 'does our Law allow a man to divorce his wife?'

Jesus answered with a question: 'What law did Moses give you?'

Their answer was: 'Moses gave permission for a man to write a divorce notice and send his wife away.'

Jesus said to them: 'Moses wrote this law for you because you are so hard to teach. But in the beginning, at the time of creation, "God made them male and female" as the scripture says. "And for this reason a man will leave his father and mother and unite with his wife, and the two will become one." So they are no longer two, but one. Man must not separate, then, what God has joined together.'

When they went back into the house, the disciples asked Jesus about this matter. He said to them: 'A man who divorces his wife and marries another woman commits adultery against his wife. In the same way, a woman who divorces her husband and marries another man commits adultery.'

(10:1–12)

In fact the Torah took divorce for granted. The real division of opinion was over what should be regarded as proper grounds for divorce.

The Pharisees take their quote out of a context of 'suppose such and such were to happen'. So they are quite right. The Torah is, in effect, giving permission for divorce to take place.

The same passage (Deuteronomy 24:1–4) says the first husband of a woman who becomes divorced for the second time, or who is made a widow by the death of her second husband, is not allowed to remarry her. 'He is to consider her defiled.' If he were to marry her again it would be 'offensive to the Lord'.

Jesus goes to another part of the Torah (Genesis 1:27) and argues from first principles.

He says that God created one single humanity, not two. The two-ness of the one people is in the two distinct sexes – male and female. It is therefore perfectly natural that they should want to come together and be together as one, because that is how God intended it right from the very beginning.

Privately, Jesus later says that while there is no law against divorce, there is certainly one against adultery – and as far as he is concerned, any marriage after divorce amounts to adultery.

FOR YOUR FOLDER

▶ Our society is very different from the one which Jesus knew. That may or may not mean that Jesus would take a different attitude if he were living today. Remember his view (as Mark reports it) is that the re-marriage of divorced persons amounts to adultery.

▶ Write down a list of all the reasons why he *should* change his mind and a list of all the reasons why he *should not*.

▶ What conclusion do you come to?

Signing the Marriage Register

THINGS TO DO

▶ Find out why some churches and Christian groups allow the re-marriage of divorced persons and why some do not.

About Fasting

On one occasion the followers of John the Baptist and the Pharisees were fasting. Some people came to Jesus and asked him: 'Why is it that the disciples of John the Baptist and the disciples of the Pharisees fast, but yours do not?'

Jesus answered: 'Do you expect the guests at a wedding party to go without food? Of course not! As long as the bridegroom is with them, they will not do that. But the day will come when the bridegroom will be taken away from them, and then they will fast.

'No-one uses a piece of new cloth to patch up an old coat, because the new patch will shrink and tear off some of the old cloth, making an even bigger hole. Nor does anyone pour new wine into used wineskins, because the wine will burst the skins, and both the wine and the skins will be ruined. Instead, new wine must be poured into fresh wineskins.'

(2:18–22)

It looks as if Mark has forgotten the bride! Maybe he has been so carried away with the idea of Jesus being the bridegroom.

The point about the wineskins is that unfermented wine needs to be put in new skins so that as the carbon dioxide is given off, the skins can expand. To use old skins, which have already been stretched, will only lead to trouble!

Jesus is saying that his approach to religion is different and you cannot just fit it into the existing patterns. Jesus tried to reform the religion of his fathers but it did not work. His approach was so fundamentally different that the skins burst and the patch tore off!

THINGS TO DO

▶ Find out why some Christians fast during Lent.

About Food

Then Jesus called the crowd to him once more and said to them: 'Listen to me, all of you, and understand. There is nothing that goes into a person from the outside which can make him ritually unclean. Rather, it is what comes out of a person that makes him unclean.'

When he left the crowd and went into the house, his disciples asked him to explain this saying. 'You are no more intelligent than the others,' Jesus said to them. 'Don't you understand? Nothing that goes into a person from the outside can really make him unclean, because it does not go into his heart but into his stomach and then goes on out of the body.' (In saying this, Jesus declared that all foods are fit to be eaten.)

And he went on to say: 'It is what comes out of a person that makes him unclean. For from the inside, from a person's heart, come the evil ideas which lead him to do immoral things, to rob, kill, commit adultery, be greedy, and do all sorts of evil things; deceit, indecency, jealousy, slander, pride, and folly – all these evil things come from inside a person and make him unclean.'

(7:14–23)

The Jewish food laws are strict and detailed. In general, however, Jews are allowed to eat:

● Any land animal that has divided hoofs and also chews the cud (provided it has been killed in the correct way and properly drained of blood).
● Any kind of fish that has fins and scales.
● Locusts, crickets and grasshoppers.
● Chicken, turkey and duck.

The whole question of food became quite an issue in the early Church and Mark's comment in brackets shows, perhaps, which side he was on!

Jesus' comment need not necessarily have been aimed at changing the food laws. He could have been simply pointing out that it is what comes out of a person in terms of words and actions that matters, not what food goes in.

Much later, Peter had a dream in which he was being invited to eat 'all kinds of animals, reptiles, and wild birds'. It made him realize that the Church should include non-Jewish Christians (Acts 10 and 11). But that did not prevent him – on one occasion at least – from choosing not to eat with the Gentile (non-Jewish) Christians (Galatians 2:11–14).

The Jerusalem Council (Acts 15) decided to write a letter to the non-Jewish Christians asking them, amongst other things, to 'eat no food that has been offered to idols; eat no blood; eat no animal that has been strangled . . .', in other words, to accept at least that amount of Jewishness.

The Christians at Corinth, who were mostly non-Jewish, told Paul in a letter that they felt perfectly free to eat whatever they liked. Paul agrees with them in principle, but says that, for his part, he would not want to use his 'freedom' to cause offence to another Christian who was far more sensitive about it than he was (1 Corinthians 8).

Mark's Gospel comes about fifteen years later.

FOR DISCUSSION

▶ What sort of challenges do Christians of today face with regard to their eating habits?

About Family

Then Jesus' mother and brothers arrived. They stood outside the house and sent in a message, asking for him. A crowd was sitting round Jesus, and they said to him: 'Look, your mother and your brothers and sisters are outside, and they want you.'

Jesus answered: 'Who is my mother? Who are my brothers?' He looked at the people sitting round him and said: 'Look! Here are my mother and my brothers! Whoever does what God wants him to do is my brother, my sister, my mother.'

(3:31–35)

There is more information about Jesus' brothers at 6:3 (see unit 23). Four are named: James, Joseph, Judas and Simon. 'Sisters' are also mentioned along with Mary. Jesus is described as 'the carpenter' and, as here, there is no mention of a father. The tradition is that Jesus took charge of the carpentry business after his father's death and waited until his brothers were old enough to take over before leaving home.

Mary and Jesus' brothers became active members of the earliest Christian community in Jerusalem (Acts 1:14) and by the time of the Jerusalem Council (see above), James had become the leader.

FOR YOUR FOLDERS

▶ How do you think Jesus' family felt about what he says here:
● At the time?
● Much later, when they were members of the Church in Jerusalem?

About Becoming a Follower

Then Jesus called the crowd and his disciples to him. 'If anyone wants to come with me,' he told

them, *'he must forget self, carry his cross, and follow me. For whoever wants to save his own life will lose it; but whoever loses his life for me and for the Gospel will save it. Does a person gain anything if he wins the whole world but loses his life? Of course not! There is nothing he can give to regain his life. If a person is ashamed of me and of my teaching in this godless and wicked day, then the Son of Man will be ashamed of him when he comes in the glory of his Father with the holy angels.'*

And he went on to say: 'I tell you, there are some here who will not die until they have seen the Kingdom of God come with power.'

(8:34–9:1)

If Jesus was prepared to suffer and die, his followers had to be ready to do the same. There was no room for those who were concerned about getting on in the world and looking after themselves.

The first generation Christians confidently expected Jesus to return quickly (see unit 34).

FOR YOUR FOLDERS

▶ What do you think Jesus means when he talks about 'life' here?

About Religious Show-offs

A large crowd was listening to Jesus gladly. As he taught them, he said: 'Watch out for the teachers of the Law, who like to walk around in their long robes and be greeted with respect in the market-place, who choose the reserved seats in the synagogues and the best places at feasts. They take advantage of widows and rob them of their homes, and then make a show of saying long prayers. Their punishment will be all the worse!'

(12:38–40)

THINGS TO DO

▶ How do you think the teachers of the Law would defend themselves against these various charges?
▶ Would Jesus have the same sort of criticisms of anyone today? Who? What makes you think so?

'Apocalyptic' is the name given to a type of literature which came into fashion among Jewish writers about two centuries before Jesus and remained popular among Jewish and Christian writers until well into the second century CE.

'Apocalyptic' means (literally) taking the lid off something – like looking in the saucepan to see how the food is coming on.

As a literary style it has certain definite features.

● The author pretends to be someone who has already lived and died. If the pseudonym was famous, nothing more need be said. If he or she was virtually unknown, a bit of a 'build-up' is needed to give them some status.

● The author first records events which have taken place both before and during the lifetime of the pseudonym. This reads as history. But it is not a straightforward history. This is because the author uses 'picture language' to describe things rather than plain words. The readers have to unravel the images and symbols to understand what is being said.

● Using the same 'coded' style, the author then 'predicts' events which have taken place before and during his or her own lifetime – but which are, of course, after the lifetime of the pseudonym. It therefore reads not as history but as a sort of prophecy. Since everything prophesied has already happened, it is seen as being 100 per cent accurate.

● Still using the same 'picture language', the author goes on to predict what will happen in the future. And since by now it is quite clear that many of the prophecies have already been fulfilled to the letter, it seems that it can only be a question of time before these other predictions also come true.

There were a great many apocalyptic books produced when the style was popular. Many of them still exist. It was a useful way of being able to say treasonable things without the occupying power realizing what was going on – an ideal way of communicating in times of persecution.

Apocalyptic ideas began to take complete control of the way that many religious people thought about the future. Some even gave up their jobs and moved to desert areas to set up monasteries where they could prepare for the coming of the new age. The Qumran community, which produced the Dead Sea Scrolls, was probably one of these.

Many early Christians believed Jesus would come back and, as it were, dance to the tune which the apocalyptists had written. In time, however, their faith matured. It changed from the raw expectation of Paul's early letters to the highly developed theology of John's Gospel.

There is not much apocalyptic literature in the Jewish Bible because it was still a fairly modern phenomenon at the time when that collection of books was being finalized. The book of Daniel, however, was included, and many of the later prophets show apocalyptic influences.

With the exception of the book of Revelation, there are no purely apocalyptic books in the New Testament part of the Christian Bible. This is partly because expectations changed and partly because the style itself had gone out of fashion by the time the final selection of books was made. But there is a great deal of apocalyptic-type thinking throughout the New Testament.

Chapter 13 in Mark has been described as the 'Little Apocalypse'.

As Jesus was leaving the Temple, one of his disciples said: 'Look Teacher! What wonderful stones and buildings!'

Jesus answered: 'You see these great buildings? Not a single stone here will be left in its place; every one of them will be thrown down.'

Jesus was sitting on the Mount of Olives, across from the Temple, when Peter, James, John, and Andrew came to him in private. 'Tell us when this will be,' they said, 'and tell us what will happen to show that the time has come for all these things to take place.'

Jesus said to them: 'Be on guard, and don't let anyone deceive you. Many men, claiming to speak for me, will come and say: "I am he!" and they will deceive many people. And don't be troubled when you hear the noise of battles close by and news of battles far away. Such things must happen, but they do not mean that the end has come. Countries will fight each other; kingdoms will attack one another. There will be earthquakes everywhere, and there will be famines. These things are like the first pains of childbirth.

'You yourselves must be on guard. You will be arrested and taken to court. You will be beaten in the synagogues; you will stand before rulers and kings for my sake to tell them the Good News. But before the end comes, the Gospel must be preached to all peoples. And when you are arrested and taken to court, do not worry beforehand about what you are going to say; when the time comes, say whatever is then given to you. For the words you speak will not be yours; they will come from the Holy Spirit. Men will hand over

their own brothers to be put to death, and fathers will do the same to their children. Children will turn against their parents and have them put to death. Everyone will hate you because of me. But whoever holds out to the end will be saved.

'You will see "The Awful Horror" standing in the place where he should not be.' (Note to the reader: be sure to understand what this means!) 'Then those who are in Judaea must run away to the hills. A man who is on the roof of his house must not lose time by going down into the house to get anything to take with him. A man who is in the field must not go back to the house for his cloak. How terrible it will be in those days for women who are pregnant and for mothers with little babies! Pray to God that these things will not happen in the winter! For the trouble of those days will be far worse than any the world has ever known from the very beginning when God created the world until the present time. Nor will there ever be anything like it again. But the Lord has reduced the number of those days; if he had not, nobody would survive. For the sake of his chosen people, however, he has reduced those days.

'Then, if anyone says to you: "Look, here is the Messiah!" or "Look, there he is!" – do not believe him. For false messiahs and false prophets will appear. They will perform miracles and wonders in order to deceive even God's chosen people, if possible. Be on your guard! I have told you everything before the time comes.

'In the days after that time of trouble, the sun will grow dark, the moon will no longer shine, the stars will fall from heaven, and the powers in space will be driven from their courses. Then the Son of Man will appear, coming in the clouds with great power and glory. He will send the angels out to the four corners of the earth to gather God's chosen people from one end of the world to the other.

'Let the fig tree teach you a lesson. When its branches become green and tender and it starts putting out leaves, you know that summer is near. In the same way, when you see these things happening, you will know that the time is near, ready to begin. Remember that all these things will happen before the people now living have all died. Heaven and earth will pass away, but my words will never pass away.

'No-one knows, however, when that day or hour will come – neither the angels in heaven, nor the Son; only the Father knows. Be on watch, be alert, for you do not know when the time will come. It will be like a man who goes away from home on a journey and leaves his servants in charge, after

giving to each one his own work to do and after telling the doorkeeper to keep watch. Be on guard, then, because you do not know when the master of the house is coming – it might be in the evening or at midnight or before dawn or at sunrise. If he comes suddenly, he must not find you asleep. What I say to you, then, I say to all: Watch!'

(13:1–37)

Work started on building Herod's Temple in 20–19 BCE but it was not finished until 62–64 CE, nearly seventy years after his death.

The phrase 'The Awful Horror' comes from the book of Daniel (9:37 etc) where it refers to the setting up of an altar to Zeus in the previous Temple by the Greek ruler Antiochus Epiphanes in 168 BCE. This action caused the Maccabean revolt which is now celebrated in the Hannukah festival each year.

In 40 CE, the Roman Emperor decided to have his statue erected in the Jerusalem Temple. The threat was not actually carried out, however, because the Proconsul sensibly delayed doing anything about it and in 41 CE the Emperor was assassinated.

In 66 CE the Roman armies moved to put down a Jewish rebellion. Jerusalem remained under seige until 70 CE when it finally surrendered to Titus. The recently completed Temple was then destroyed.

FOR YOUR FOLDERS

▶ Using the above information, say when do you think this 'Little Apocalypse' in Mark was written. Give reasons for your answer.
▶ What evidence is there in Mark's Gospel to show that the early Christians found it difficult to accept that Jesus was not the sort of Messiah the apocalyptic books were expecting?

THINGS TO DO

▶ Find out about Qumran and the Dead Sea Scrolls.
▶ The Jehovah's Witnesses say the events predicted here (and in Daniel and Revelation) will happen one day in the future. Find out more about what they believe.

The Temple

The name given to each area of the Temple identified the people who stopped there and went no further. At the point where the Court of the Gentiles became the Court of the Women, for example, there was a notice which warned non-Jews that if they went further they could be arrested and put to death. The other areas were the Court of the Israelites, the Court of the Priests and, finally, the Holy of Holies.

QUICK QUIZ

▶ Can you remember who went into the Holy of Holies and when? If not, look it up in unit 11.

The Court of the Gentiles was used all year round to sell the animals for sacrifice and for money-changing. At this time of the year it would have been particularly busy dealing with the pilgrims who had come from all over the then-known world for Passover.

They would have had to change their Roman money into Temple money, otherwise they would be taking images of heathen gods into the holy place. The money-changers were able to charge a high rate of exchange and all the profits went to the chief priests.

The pilgrims would also be buying whatever animals or birds they needed for Temple sacrifices, as well as ordering their Passover lamb.

When they arrived in Jerusalem, Jesus went to the Temple and began to drive out all those who were buying and selling. He overturned the tables of the money-changers and the stools of those who sold pigeons, and he would not let anyone carry anything through the Temple courtyards. He then taught the people: 'It is written in the Scriptures that God said: "My Temple will be called a house of prayer for the people of all nations." But you have turned it into a hideout for thieves!'

The chief priests and the teachers of the Law heard of this, so they began looking for some way to kill Jesus. They were afraid of him, because the whole crowd was amazed at his teaching.

When evening came, Jesus and his disciples left the city.

(11:15–19)

Clearing the Court of the Gentiles

In his entry into the city (see unit 18), Jesus had been fulfilling Zechariah's prophecy. In entering the Temple, Mark sees him as fulfilling Malachi 3:1: '. . . the Lord you are looking for will suddenly come to his Temple.'

Once into the Court of the Gentiles, Jesus set about clearing the traders out, claiming the words of Isaiah (56:7) and Jeremiah (7:11) as his authority.

The problem for the chief priests and the teachers of the Law was that Jesus was absolutely right to do what he did – and they knew it! This part of the Temple was meant to be available for non-Jewish people and the authorities themselves were preventing them from using it.

Jesus had been challenging the Pharisees and others in the synagogues of Galilee to have a new approach to what it meant to live in God's way. Now he had come to Jerusalem and was challenging the priests, in the Temple itself.

In Galilee it had all been reasonably remote as far as the Temple authorities were concerned; in Jerusalem their power-base was being threatened. Jesus was putting his head into the lion's mouth – and the lion was getting angry!

THINGS TO DO

▶ Imagine it is evening. Jesus and the disciples have left the city and have gone back to where they are staying. Two or three of them are discussing the day's events. Write a suitable script.

What Right Have You . . . ?

They arrived once again in Jerusalem. As Jesus was walking in the Temple, the chief priests, the teachers of the Law and the elders came to him and asked him: 'What right have you to do these things? Who gave you this right?'

Jesus answered them: 'I will ask you just one question, and if you give me an answer, I will tell you what right I have to do these things. Tell me, where did John's right to baptize come from: was it from God or from man?'

They started to argue among themselves: 'What shall we say? If we answer: "From God," he will say: "Why, then, did you not believe John?" But if we say: "From man . . ."' (They were afraid of the people, because everyone was convinced that

John had been a prophet.) So their answer to Jesus was: 'We don't know.'

Jesus said to them: 'Neither will I tell you, then, by what right I do these things.'

(11:27–33)

FOR YOUR FOLDERS

▶ Is Jesus claiming to be the Messiah without saying so in as many words? Give reasons for your answer. Refer to unit 18 if you need to.

▶ If Jesus had decided to give a straight answer to a straight question, what do you think his answer would have been?

The Story of the Vineyard

Then Jesus spoke to them in parables: 'Once there was a man who planted a vineyard, put a fence round it, dug a hole for the winepress, and built a watch-tower. Then he let out the vineyard to tenants and left home on a journey. When the time came to gather the grapes, he sent a slave to the tenants to receive from them his share of the harvest. The tenants seized the slave, beat him, and sent him back without a thing. Then the owner sent another slave; the tenants beat him over the head and treated him shamefully. The owner sent another slave, and they killed him; and they treated many others the same way, beating some and killing others. The only one left to send was the man's own dear son. Last of all, then, he sent his son to the tenants. "I am sure they will respect my son," he said. But those tenants said to one another: "This is the owner's son. Come on, let's kill him, and his property will be ours!" So they seized the son and killed him and threw his body out of the vineyard.

'What, then, will the owner of the vineyard do?' asked Jesus. 'He will come and kill those men and hand the vineyard over to other tenants. Surely you have read this scripture?

"The stone which the builders rejected as worthless
turned out to be the most important of all.
This was done by the Lord;
what a wonderful sight it is!"

The Jewish leaders tried to arrest Jesus, because they knew that he had told this parable against them. But they were afraid of the crowd, so they left him and went away.

(12:1–12)

Isaiah's 'Song of the Vineyard', written some 700 years earlier, must have provided the raw material for what Jesus had to say:

Listen while I sing you this song,
a song of my friend and his vineyard:
My friend had a vineyard
on a very fertile hill.
He dug the soil and cleared it of stones;
he planted the finest vines.
He built a tower to guard them,
dug a pit for treading the grapes.
He waited for the grapes to ripen,
but every grape was sour.

So now my friend says: 'You people who live in Jerusalem and Judah, judge between my vineyard and me. Is there anything I failed to do for it? Then why did it produce sour grapes and not the good grapes I expected? This is what I am going to do to my vineyard; I will take away the hedge round it, break down the wall that protects it, and let wild animals eat it and trample it down. I will let it be overgrown with weeds. I will not prune the vines or hoe the ground; instead I will let briars and thorns cover it. I will even forbid the clouds to let rain fall on it.'

Israel is the vineyard of the Lord Almighty;
the people of Judah are the vines he planted.
He expected them to do what was good,
but instead they committed murder.
He expected them to do what was right,
but their victims cried out for justice.

(Isaiah 5:1–7)

QUICK QUIZ

▶ The story in Mark appears to be an allegory rather than a parable. What is an allegory? (See unit 28.) What does the vineyard represent? Who is the owner? Who are the tenants? Who are the slaves? Who is the son? When did the owner do what Jesus said he would do?

FOR YOUR FOLDERS

▶ Do you think this is the original story as told by Jesus or is it one which has been developed by the early Church? What evidence can you find to support your answer?

Question About Taxes

Some Pharisees and some members of Herod's party were sent to Jesus to trap him with questions. They came to him and said: 'Teacher, we know that you tell the truth, without worrying about what people think. You pay no attention to a man's status, but teach the truth about God's will for man. Tell us, is it against our Law to pay taxes to the Roman Emperor? Should we pay them or not?'

But Jesus saw through their trick and answered: 'Why are you trying to trap me? Bring me a silver coin, and let me see it.'

They brought him one, and he asked: 'Whose face and name are these?'

'The Emperor's,' they answered.

So Jesus said: 'Well, then pay the Emperor what belongs to the Emperor, and pay God what belongs to God.'

And they were amazed at Jesus.

(12:13–17)

Quakers at worship

The Houses of Parliament, where British taxes are set

If the Pharisees were the major religious party, the Herodians were the major political party among the Jews.

Jews had to pay two taxes, one to Rome and one to the Temple. The question to Jesus was an 'either/or' one; his answer was a 'both/and' one. Since Herod's party approved of the one and the Pharisees approved of the other, neither could take offence.

No wonder they were amazed!

THINGS TO DO

▶ Some Quakers have chosen to go to prison for withholding that part of their taxes which is used to pay for the upkeep of the armed forces in general and nuclear weapons in particular. What do you think Jesus would say to them?

Question About Resurrection

Then some Sadducees, who say that people will not rise from death, came to Jesus and said: 'Teacher, Moses wrote this law for us: "If a man dies and leaves a wife but no children, that man's brother must marry the widow so that they can have children who will be considered the dead man's children." Once there were seven brothers; the eldest got married and died without having children. Then the second one married the woman, and he also died without having children. The same thing happened to the third brother, and then to the rest: all seven brothers married the woman and died without having children. Last of all, the woman died. Now, when all the dead rise to life on the day of Resurrection, whose wife will she be? All seven of them had married her.'

Jesus answered them: 'How wrong you are! And do you know why? It is because you don't know the Scriptures or God's power. For when the dead rise to life, they will be like the angels in heaven and will not marry. Now, as for the dead being raised: haven't you ever read in the Book of Moses the passage about the burning bush? There it is written that God said to Moses: "I am the God of Abraham, the God of Isaac, and the God of Jacob." He is the God of the living, not of the dead. You are completely wrong!'

(12:18–27)

The Pharisees believed in a general resurrection at the end of the age; the Sadducees did not. Their difference in belief was because of their different attitude to the Torah.

The Pharisees said they were prepared to accept ideas and beliefs which seemed reasonable if the Torah did not specifically say they were wrong.

The Sadducees said they were not prepared to accept any ideas or beliefs, however reasonable they seemed, if the Torah did not specifically say they were right.

The idea of a general resurrection at the end of the age was just such an idea. The Torah said nothing specific about it.

Jesus says marriage belongs to this age, not to the age to come.

But he also points out, quoting from the Torah (Exodus 3:6), that if God claimed to be ('I am') the God of three generations who, as far as Moses was concerned, were all dead and buried, it must mean they were living and not dead.

FOR DISCUSSION

▶ Who do you think Jesus had more in common with – the Pharisees or the Sadducees? Why?

Question About the Most Important commandment

A teacher of the Law was there who heard the discussion. He saw that Jesus had given the Sadducees a good answer, so he came to him with a question: 'Which commandment is the most important of all?'

Jesus replied: 'The most important one is this: "Listen Israel! The Lord our God is the only Lord. Love the Lord your God with all your heart, with all your soul, with all your mind, and with all your strength." The second most important commandment is this: "Love your neighbour as you love yourself." There is no other commandment more important than these two.'

The teacher of the Law said to Jesus: 'Well done, Teacher! It is true, as you say, that only the Lord is God and that there is no other god but he. And man must love God with all his heart and with all his mind and with all his strength; and he must love his neighbour as he loves himself. It is more important to obey these two commandments than to offer animals and other sacrifices to God.'

Jesus noticed how wise his answer was, and so he told him: 'You are not far from the Kingdom of God.'

After this nobody dared to ask Jesus any more questions.

(12:28–34)

The Torah contains 613 commands – 248 positive ('do's') and 365 negative ('don'ts').

For Jesus, they were all summed up in the words of the Shema (Deuteronomy 6:4–5) about loving God and the command (Leviticus 19:18) about loving one's neighbour as oneself.

There are at least three Greek words which are translated by the single English word 'love'. This one is 'agape'. Unlike *'erotic'* and *'phil*-anthrop-*ic'*, *'agape'* does not have an English equivalent. It means 'to have the highest regard and the deepest concern'.

The teacher of the Law agrees. He adds that obeying these two commandments is more important even than the Temple rituals, a reminder of the words of Micah which many feel express the heart of the Jewish religion:

'. . . the Lord has told us what is good. What he requires of us is this: to do what is just, to show constant love, and to live in humble fellowship with our God.'

(Micah 6:8)

FOR YOUR FOLDERS

▶ What do you think Jesus meant when he told this teacher of the Law: 'You are not far from the Kingdom of God'?

TEST YOURSELF!

1 What did Jesus say at the Last Supper about the wine and the Kingdom of God?
2 When did Jesus say: 'The right time has come and the Kingdom of God is near!'?
3 What are the two meanings of the word 'parable'?
4 There are two parables about the Kingdom of God in Mark's Gospel. Recount one of them briefly.

5 What is an allegory?
6 There were four types of ground in the allegory of the sower. What were they?
7 What did these four types of ground represent?
8 What point was Jesus trying to make?
9 What trade did the first two followers of Jesus have?
10 Name another four disciples.
11 What did Jesus do and say when he discovered that the disciples had been arguing about who was the greatest among them?
12 To whom did Jesus say the Kingdom of God 'belonged'?
13 The man who had obeyed all the commandments ever since he was young needed only one thing to receive eternal life. What was it?
14 What does 'eternal life' mean?
15 What did Jesus say was 'impossible for man, but not for God'?

16 What did James and John want from Jesus?
17 What did he ask them in reply?
18 What did Jesus say should be the pattern of relationships between his followers?
19 What reason did he give?
20 What attitude did Jesus say the disciples should take to other people who were doing things in his name?
21 Why did he say they should take this attitude?
22 Jesus gave some very graphic descriptions of making sure one was spiritually ready for the Kingdom of God. Outline one of them.
23 There are three 'salt' sayings in Mark's Gospel. Give one of them.
24 What did Jesus say about the poor widow who dropped two little copper coins into the Temple treasury?

25 What did Jesus say to the Pharisees who asked why he was eating with tax collectors and other outcasts?
26 Jesus called the Pharisees 'hypocrites' when they questioned him as to why his disciples did not wash their hands before eating. What does 'hypocrite' mean?
27 Why did he call them hypocrites?
28 What did Jesus say about the Sabbath, man and the Son of Man?
29 What led up to his saying this?
30 Why did Jesus say Moses had given permission for divorce?
31 What was Jesus' attitude to divorce and re-marriage?

32 What was Jesus' response to those people who asked him why his disciples were not observing a fast?
33 What evidence is there in Mark's Gospel to suggest that Jesus did not expect his followers to remain part of Judaism?
34 What according to Jesus made a person 'unclean', if it was not what they ate?
35 Who did Jesus say was his brother, his sister and his mother?
36 Jesus said if anyone wanted to follow him, they should forget something and remember to bring something. What were these things?
37 Why did Jesus say they should 'watch out for the teachers of the Law'?

38 What does 'apocalyptic' mean?
39 What are the four distinguishing features of apocalyptic literature?
40 What sort of things had happened generally in the world at large from the time of Jesus to the time that Chapter 13 was written?
41 What was happening in Jerusalem at the time Chapter 13 was written?
42 What were the followers of Jesus to be on their guard against?
43 When would the end of the age come?

44 Why did Jesus clear out the Court of the Gentiles?
45 What was the reaction of the authorities?
46 What question was Jesus asked and what question did he ask in reply, to cause the questioners to say: 'We don't know'?
47 What was Jesus saying in the parable of the vineyard?
48 To whom did Jesus say the people should pay taxes?
49 Did Jesus agree with the Pharisees or the Sadducees regarding the idea of resurrection at the end of the age?
50 Why did Jesus say the teacher of the Law was 'not far from the Kingdom of God'?

**Part 5
OTHER MATTERS**

It is important – especially if you are taking an examination – to have a very clear idea of the actual order in which things come in the Gospel.

This unit is designed to help you:

Description	Reference	Unit
Title verse:	1:1	40
John the Baptist in the desert:	1:2–8	17
Baptism of Jesus:	1:9–13	19
Jesus comes to Galilee:	1:14–15	27
First disciples:	1:16–20	29
Man in the synagogue:	1:21–28	20
Simon's mother-in-law healed:	1:29–31	22
Summary of healings:	1:32–34	21
Making time for prayer	1:35–39	21
Man with skin disease healed:	1:40–45	22
Paralyzed man healed:	2:1–12	24
Levi becomes a disciple:	2:13–17	31
Question of fasting:	2:18–22	33
Working on the Sabbath?:	2:23–28	32
Healing on the Sabbath:	3:1–6	24
Summary of healings:	3:7–12	21
Twelve apostles:	3:13–19	29
Jesus and Beelzebul:	3:20–30	21
Jesus and his family:	3:31–35	33
Parable of the sower:	4:1–9	28
Parables as riddles:	4:10–12	27
Meaning of the 'parable':	4:13–25	28
Parables of the Kingdom:	4:26–34	27
Storm on the lake:	4:35–41	26
Healing of 'Mob':	5:1–20	20
Healing of woman in the crowd:	5:21–34	22
Healing of Jairus' daughter:	5:35–43	22
Rejected at Nazareth:	6:1–6	23
Twelve disciples sent out:	6:7–13	21
Death of John the Baptist:	6:14–29	17
Feeding of the 5,000:	6:30–44	25
Jesus walks on the water:	6:45–52	25
Summary of healings:	6:53–56	23
Traditions of the Pharisees:	7:1–13	31
Real uncleanliness:	7:14–23	33
Syro-Phoenician woman's daughter:	7:24–30	21
Healing of deaf and dumb man:	7:31–37	23
Feeding of the 4,000:	8:1–10	25
Pharisees want a miracle:	8:11–13	21
Yeast of the Pharisees, etc:	8:14–21	25
Healing blind man at Bethsaida:	8:22–26	23
Caesarea Philippi:	8:27–33	16

Description	Reference	Unit
First prediction of suffering:	8:34–9:1	33
Transfiguration:	9:2–9	19
Elijah's coming	9:10–13	17
Healing of the epileptic boy:	9:14–29	20
Second prediction of suffering:	9:30–32	16
Question of greatness:	9:33–37	29
Question of competition:	9:38–41	30
Getting rid of hindrances:	9:42–50	30
Divorce and marriage:	10:1–12	32
Child-like attitude wanted:	10:13–16	29
Rich people and the Kingdom:	10:17–31	29
Third prediction of suffering:	10:32–34	16
Question of rewards:	10:35–45	30
Healing of Bartimaeus:	10:46–52	24
Entry into Jerusalem:	11:1–6	18
Fig tree cursed:	11:12–14	26
Clearing out the Temple:	11:15–19	35
Fig tree and prayer:	11:20–26	26
Question of authority:	11:27–33	35
Story of the vineyard:	12:1–12	35
Question of paying taxes:	12:13–17	36
Question about resurrection:	12:18–27	36
Question about commandment:	12:28–34	36
Son of David?:	12:35–37	18
Beware of show-offs:	12:38–40	33
The widow's gift:	12:41–44	30
The future:	13:1–37	34

Starting With John

The prophet Malachi predicted that before the Messiah came, Elijah will have returned. Mark starts his Gospel with John, because he believes that John is Elijah. Along with many others, Jesus is baptized by John and confirmed as the Servant-Messiah who must suffer and die. Satan tests him in the desert.

In Galilee

When John has been put in prison by Herod, Jesus begins to preach publicly in Galilee the coming of God's Kingdom. Four fishermen become his first disciples. He teaches 'with authority' in the synagogue at Capernaum and carries out an exorcism on a man who screams out in the middle of the service. Later, he cures Simon's mother-in-law of a fever. By evening a large crowd has gathered and Jesus is kept busy curing the sick people. But he is up before dawn the next morning because he wants time to be alone in prayer.

He and his disciples travel all over the Galilee

region. He heals a man with a dreaded skin disease by touching him. He heals a paralyzed man by convincing him that his sins are forgiven. He asks a tax collector to become one of his disciples and he quite deliberately has a lot to do with people who are shunned by other religious teachers.

People notice the difference in the way Jesus and his disciples behave. They do not fast, nor do they keep the sabbath strictly. Jesus responds to human need wherever and whenever he can – even in the synagogue on the sabbath. By now, people are coming from all over the country to hear Jesus and to be healed by him.

Jesus chooses twelve of his followers with a view to sending them out to preach and drive out demons. The teachers of the Law accuse Jesus of practising black magic but he refutes them with some logical thinking. He refuses to go home, on the grounds that he belongs to a much larger family. He talks to people in parables. Those who share the 'secret' of the kingdom of God know exactly what he means: for the rest it is all riddles.

Jesus and his disciples cross Lake Galilee. On the way, Jesus calms a storm on the lake. Once he arrives in the territory of Gerasa, Jesus calms the 'storm' which has been raging in Mob's life. On his return, a woman only has to touch him to be cured, and a little girl is brought back to life when Jesus speaks to her.

The people of Jesus' home town of Nazareth reject him but this does not surprise him greatly 'because the people did not have faith'. Jesus sends out the twelve having told them how to react to different situations. About this time John is beheaded by Herod – an action replay of the Elijah-Jezebel-Ahab story.

When the 'apostles' return, Jesus takes them to the other side of the lake, but the crowds follow. Like Moses before him, Jesus feeds them in the desert. Later, Jesus joins the disciples as they are crossing the lake by boat. Everywhere Jesus goes he brings healing and, not surprizingly, he is in constant demand.

Some Pharisees and teachers of the Law ask why some of Jesus' disciples do not ritually wash their hands before eating. He says that the question of whether people are good or bad does not depend on what they eat or how they eat it. A non-Jewish woman begs Jesus to heal her daughter and tells him that even the 'dogs' can eat the children's scraps from the table. When she goes home she finds that her daughter is well. Another healing in a gentile area is that of the man who was deaf and dumb.

Jesus now feeds 4,000 people on the other side of the lake – or is this a double of the other story when he fed 5,000 people? His disciples have difficulty in 'seeing' what he means and the blind man at Bethsaida gets his sight back in stages. Peter thinks that he sees things very clearly. 'You are the Messiah', he says to Jesus. But he cannot yet see that this must mean Jesus suffering and dying. The disciples are beginning to see Jesus in a new light. The Law and the Prophets, the twin pillars of Judaism, fade away in the light of the transfigured Jesus. Back on ground level, that the disciples still need plenty of faith and prayer.

Towards Jerusalem

The disciples still do not understand Jesus when he talks about his coming death and resurrection. They spend their time arguing about who is the greatest and whether other exorcists are friends or enemies. Jesus calls for humility and spiritual readiness. He shows that he does not approve of divorce and that he loves having children around. Spiritual problems come when people love things like money.

For the third time, Jesus spells out exactly what will befall him. James and John want prestige. The way to that, says Jesus, is through the self-denial that comes with servanthood. Bartimaeus wants his sight and he gets it – because of his faith.

In Jerusalem

Jesus rides into Jerusalem as the King of Peace. He gets rid of three things: the tradespeople who are in the Court of the Gentiles; a fig tree which is not fulfilling its intended purpose; those who question his authority. He tells a story about a vineyard in which the owner's son is murdered by the tenants – and guess who he thinks the 'tenants' are!

Jesus says that both the Emperor and God should receive what is due to them. He shows the Sadducees that he sides with the Pharisees on the question of resurrection; and he sums up the Law, in terms of love to God and one's fellow human beings. He then shows that he disagrees with the idea that the Messiah must be 'Son of David', that he disapproves of religious show-offs, and that he regards real giving as that which hurts the purse or pocket.

For Chapter 13 see Unit 34. The remaining chapters of the Gospel (14:1 to 16:20) are dealt with in sequence in Units 3 to 13.

38 PUTTING IT ON THE MAP

THINGS TO DO

▶ You can find out what happened in each of the various places on the map by comparing the events in this list of quotations with the list of bible references in the previous unit. Prepare some questions to test your friends. For example:

● *Where did Jesus heal the man in the synagogue?*
● *Where was Jesus when he was asked the question about paying taxes?*
● *Where was 'Mob' healed?*
● *Where did Jesus first talk about how he was going to suffer and die?*

Make sure you will be able to answer any questions that your friends will be asking you!

▶ There is one place mentioned which does not appear on the map. It is thought that it must be a copyist's error because the place just does not – and never did – exist. What is the name of the place?

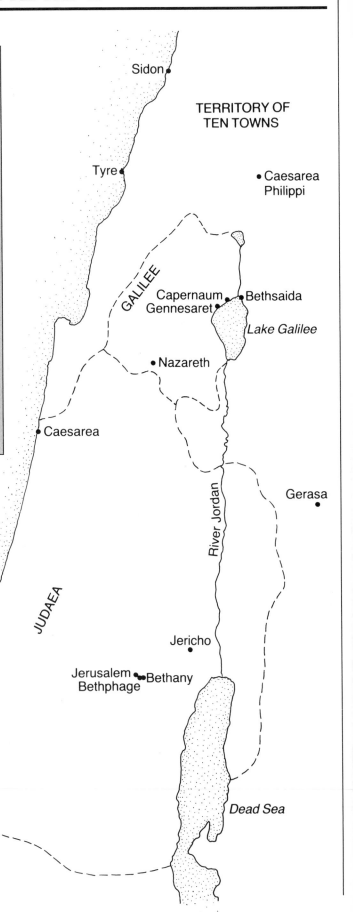

John appeared in the desert, baptizing and preaching. . . . Many people from the province of Judaea and the city of Jerusalem went out to hear John. They confessed their sins and he baptized them in the River Jordan. (1:4–5)

Not long afterwards Jesus came from Nazareth in the province of Galilee, and was baptized by John in the Jordan. (1:9)

At once the spirit made him go into the desert, where he stayed forty days, being tempted by Satan. (1:12)

After John had been put in prison, Jesus went to Galilee . . . . (1:14)

As Jesus walked along the shore of Lake Galilee . . . . (1:16)

Jesus and his disciples came to the town of Capernaum . . . . (1:21)

. . . he travelled all over Galilee . . . . (1:39)

A few days later Jesus went back to Capernaum, and the news spread that he was at home. (2:1)

Jesus and his disciples arrived on the other side of Lake Galilee, in the territory of Gerasa. (5:1)

Jesus went back across to the other side of the lake. (5:21)

Jesus left that place and went back to his home town, followed by his disciples. (6:1)

Then Jesus went to the villages round there, teaching the people. (6:6b)

(The Twelve) . . . went out and preached . . . (6:12)

(The Twelve) . . . returned and met with Jesus . . . . (6:30)

. . . they started out in a boat by themselves for a lonely place. (6:32)

They crossed the lake and came to land at Gennesaret . . . . (6:53)

Then Jesus left and went away to the territory near the city of Tyre. (7:24)

Jesus then left the neighbourhood of Tyre and went on through Sidon to Lake Galilee, going by way of the territory of the Ten Towns. (7:31)

Jesus . . . got into a boat with his disciples and went to the district of Dalmanutha. (8:10)

He . . . got back into the boat, and started across to the other side of the lake. (8:13)

They came to Bethsaida . . . . (8:22)

Then Jesus and his disciples went away to the villages near Caesarea Philippi . . . . (8:27)

Jesus and his disciples left that place and went on through Galilee. (9:30)

They came to Capernaum . . . . (9:33)

Then Jesus left that place, went to the province of Judaea, and crossed the River Jordan. (10:1)

Jesus and his disciples were now on the road going up to Jerusalem. (10:32)

They came to Jericho . . . . (10:46)

As they approached Jerusalem, near the towns of Bethphage and Bethany, they came to the Mount of Olives. (11:1)

Jesus entered Jerusalem, went into the Temple, and looked round at everything. But since it was already late in the day, he went out to Bethany with the twelve disciples. The next day, as they were coming back from Bethany . . . . (11:11–12a)

When they arrived in Jerusalem, Jesus went to the Temple . . . . (11:15)

When evening came, Jesus and his disciples left the city. Early next morning as they walked along the road . . . . (11:19–20a)

They arrived once again in Jerusalem. As Jesus was walking in the Temple . . . . (11:27)

As Jesus was leaving the Temple . . . (13:1)

Jesus was in Bethany . . . . (14:3)

(On the first day of the Festival) . . . when it was evening, Jesus came (to Jerusalem) with the twelve disciples. (14:17)

Matthew and Luke have a lot more information than Mark on what Jesus said and did, but most experts are convinced that they both used Mark as a basic outline for their own Gospels. The three are called the Synoptists because they 'look at things together'. While a study of Mark's Gospel is not a study of either or both these other two Gospels, it is sometimes quite useful to look at the similarities and differences between them.

To help you to do this, here are the chapter and verse details of where you will find the equivalent passages in Matthew and Luke.

Mark	Matthew	Luke
1:1–8	3:1–12	3:1–18
1:9–11	3:13–17	3:21–23
1:12–13	4:1–11	4:1–15
1:14–20	4:12–22	5:1–11
1:21–28	–	4:31–37
1:29–34	8:14–17	4:38–41
1:35–39	–	4:42–44
1:40–45	8:1–4	5:12–16
2:1–12	9:1–8	5:17–26
2:13–17	9:9–13	5:27–32
2:18–22	9:14–17	5:33–39
2:23–28	12:1–8	6:1–5
3:1–6	12:9–14	6:6–11
3:7–12	4:23–25	6:17–19
3:13–19	10:1–4	6:12–16
3:20–30	12:22–45	11:14–32
3:31–35	12:46–50	8:19–21
4:1–9	13:1–9	8:4–8
4:10–12	13:10–17	8:9–10
4:13–20	13:18–23	8:11–15
4:21–23	5:13–16	8:16–18
4:24–25	7:1–6	6:37–42
4:26–29	–	–
4:30–34	13:31–32 and 34	13:18–19
4:35–41	8:23–27	8:22–25
5:1–20	8:28–34	8:26–39
5:21–43	9:18–26	8:40–56
6:1–6	13:53–58	4:16–30
6:7–15 and 30	10:1 and 5–15	9:1–10
6:14–29	14:1–12	9:7–9
6:31–44	14:13–21	9:10–17
6:45–56	14:22–36	–
7:1–23	15:1–20	–
7:24–30	15:21–31	–
7:31–37	–	–
8:1–10	15:29–39	–

Mark	Matthew	Luke
8:11–13	12:38–42 or 16:1–4	11:29–32 or 12:54–56
8:14–21	16:5–12	–
8:22–26	–	–
8:27–30	16:13–20	9:18–21
8:31–9:1	16:21–28	9:22–27
9:2–13	17:1–13	9:28–36
9:14–29	17:14–21	9:37–43
9:30–32	17:22–23	9:43–45
9:33–37	18:1–5	9:46–48
9:38–41	–	9:49–50
9:42–50	18:6–9	17:1–2
10:1–12	19:1–12	16:18
10:13–16	19:13–15	18:15–17
10:17–31	19:16–30	18:18–30
10:32–34	20:17–19	18:31–34
10:35–45	20:20–28	–
10:46–52	20:29–34	18:35–43
11:1–11	21:1–11	19:28–40
11:12–14 and 20–25	21:18–22	–
11:15–19	21:12–17	19:45–48
11:27–33	21:23–27	20:1–8
12:1–12	21:33–46	20:9–19
12:13–17	22:15–22	20:20–26
12:18–27	22:23–33	20:27–40
12:28–34	22:34–40	10:25–28
12:35–37	22:41–46	20:41–44
12:38–40	23:1–36	20:45–47
12:41–44	–	21:1–4
13:1–31	24:1–35	21:5–33
14:1–2	26:1–5	22:1–2
14:3–9	26:6–13	–
14:10–11	26:14–16	22:3–6
14:12–21	26:17–25	22:7–14
14:22–26	26:26–30	22:14–20
14:27–31	26:31–35	22:31–34
14:32–42	26:36–46	22:39–46
14:43–52	26:47–56	22:47–53
14:53–72	26:57–75	22:54–71
15:1–5	27:1–2 and 11–14	23:1–5
15:6–15	27:15–26	23:13–25
15:16–20	27:27–31	–
15:21–32	27:32–44	23:26–43
15:33–41	27:45–56	23:44–49
15:42–47	27:57–61	23:50–56
16:1–8	28:1–8	24:1–12
16:9–20	(see unit 14)	

You will see from the table opposite that there are three passages which are 'peculiar' to Mark. This means that Matthew and Luke do not use them and they do not appear anywhere else in the New Testament. If both the other Gospel writers were using Mark's Gospel as a framework for their own, there must be some good reason for their leaving these passages out.

The three passages are: the parable of the growing seed, the healing of the deaf man in the territory of the Ten Towns, and the healing of the blind man at Bethsaida.

In the case of the two healings, these come in a much larger section which Luke seems to omit deliberately (from 6:45 to 8:26). He has the Pharisees asking for some proof (Mark 8:11–13) later on in chapters 11 or 12.

This could also explain why both Luke and Matthew leave out the parable of the growing seed. Each of them is 'out of sequence' with Mark at the time and both could have overlooked it. They have plenty of parables in any case, far more than Mark has.

In the case of the two healings, however, Matthew apparently makes a quite deliberate decision to exclude them from his Gospel.

Jesus went on to say, 'The Kingdom of God is like this. A man scatters seed in his field. He sleeps at night, is up and about during the day, and all the while the seeds are sprouting and growing. Yet he does not know how it happens. The soil itself makes the plants grow and bear fruit; first the tender stalk appears, then the ear, and finally the ear full of corn. When the corn is ripe, the man starts cutting it with his sickle, because harvest time has come.'

(4:26–29)

Jesus then left the neighbourhood of Tyre and went on through Sidon to Lake Galilee, going by way of the territory of the Ten Towns. Some people brought him a man who was deaf and could hardly speak, and they begged Jesus to place his hands on him. So Jesus took him off alone, away from the crowd, put his fingers in the man's ears, spat, and then touched the man's tongue. Then Jesus looked up to heaven, gave a deep groan, and said to the man, 'Ephphatha', which means, 'Open up!'
At once the man was able to hear, his speech impediment was removed, and he began to talk without any trouble. Then Jesus ordered the people not to speak of it to anyone; but the more
he ordered them not to, the more they spoke. And all who heard were completely amazed. 'How well he does everything!' they exclaimed. 'He even causes the deaf to hear and the dumb to speak!'

(7:31–37)

They came to Bethsaida, where some people brought a blind man to Jesus and begged him to touch him. Jesus took the blind man by the hand and led him out of the village. After spitting on the man's eyes, Jesus placed his hands on him and asked him, 'Can you see anything?'
The man looked up and said, 'Yes, I can see people, but they look like trees walking about'
Jesus again placed his hands on the man's eyes. This time the man looked intently, his eyesight returned, and he saw everything clearly. Jesus then sent him home with the order, 'Don't go back into the village.'

(8:22–26)

FOR DISCUSSION

▶ Why do you think these two healings were deliberately left out of Matthew's Gospel? Is there anything about the stories which may not have presented Jesus in the best possible light? Do you think these things might make it more likely that the stories are in fact genuine?

FOR YOUR FOLDERS

▶ Compare and contrast these three verses:
Mark 6:39
Matthew 14:19
Luke 9:14
Which seems to you to be the words of an eyewitness?
▶ Compare and contrast Mark 6:45–56 with Matthew 14:22–36. If Mark was the one who wrote down the things which Peter remembered (see unit 40), why do you think he has forgotten to include *this* story about Peter, which only Matthew, out of all the Gospel writers, has recorded? Or is *this* saying something about Matthew rather than Mark?

Who Wrote the Gospel?

Eusebius, Bishop of Caesarea, wrote a history of the Church in the early part of the fourth century CE. In it, he quotes from the earlier work of Papias who was Bishop of Hierapolis in about 130 CE.

> (John) the Elder used to say this also: Mark became the interpreter of Peter and he wrote down accurately, but not in order, as much as he remembered (or related) of the sayings and doings of the Lord . . . .

Eusebius also quotes from Irenaeus, Bishop of Lyons, who wrote in about 185 CE:

> Matthew published his Gospel among the Hebrews in their own tongue, when Peter and Paul were preaching the Gospel in Rome and founding the church there. After their departure Mark, the disciple and interpreter of Peter, himself handed down to us in writing the substance of Peter's preaching.

St Mark's Cathedral, Venice

The early Church was quite sure that this Gospel had been written by Mark. The overwhelming majority of experts today also agree that this Mark must have been the John Mark mentioned in the early Christian letters and writings:

> (After his escape from prison in Jerusalem) Peter went to the home of Mary, the mother of John Mark, where many people had gathered and were praying.
>
> (Acts 12:12)

> Barnabas and Saul (Paul) (who had been in Jerusalem for the Council) finished their mission and returned from Jerusalem, taking John Mark with them.
>
> (Acts 12:25)

> Some time later Paul said to Barnabas: 'Let us go back and visit our brothers in every town where we preached the word of the Lord, and let us find out how they are getting on.' Barnabas wanted to take John Mark with them, but Paul did not think it was right to take him, because he had not stayed with them to the end of their mission but had turned back and left them in Pamphylia. There was a sharp argument, and they separated: Barnabas took Mark and sailed off for Cyprus . . . .
>
> (Acts 15:36–39)

> Aristarchus, who is in prison with me, sends you greetings, and so does Mark, the cousin of Barnabas. (You have already received instructions to welcome Mark if he comes your way.) Joshua, also called Justus, sends greetings too. These three are the only Jewish believers who work with me for the Kingdom of God, and they have been a great help to me.
>
> (Paul's letter to the Colossians 4:10–11)

> Epaphras, who is in prison with me for the sake of Christ Jesus, sends you his greetings, and so do my fellow workers Mark, Aristarchus, Demas and Luke.
>
> (Paul's letter to Philemon 23–24)

> Only Luke is with me. Get Mark and bring him with you, because he can help me in the work.
>
> (Paul's second letter to Timothy 4:11)

THINGS TO DO

▶ You now have all the references to Mark in the Christian Bible and in other early Christian writings (you will also have to decide about the nameless young man who ran away when Jesus was arrested – see unit 6 – and the nameless young man who was at the empty tomb – see unit 13).

Write a 250-word profile on Mark which could be used on the back cover of a paperback edition of his Gospel.

When was the Gospel Written?

There is a very strong tradition that Peter and Paul were put to death in the persecution of Christians which followed the fire of Rome in 64 CE. The Emperor Nero was suspected of causing this fire which destroyed a large part of the city, but he fixed the responsibility on the Christians. Nero himself committed suicide in 68 CE.

Why was the Gospel Written?

Peter would have been in his late sixties or early seventies when he was put to death. It was now some thirty-five years after the Crucifixion and those who had actually known Jesus would not be around for ever. The expectation that Jesus would return very shortly (see unit 34) was gradually fading and people were beginning to take a longer-term view.

Churches and Christian communities were beginning to feel the need for the stories to be written down rather than being passed on by word of mouth all the time. Christianity was no longer just in one small city; it was to be found in all the major towns and cities of the Roman Empire. A written record was becoming more and more necessary.

But there were more reasons than simply the practical one of needing a record for future generations. The title page of Mark's Gospel, as it were, is as follows:

> This is the Good News about Jesus Christ, the Son of God.
>
> (1:1)

Mark's main purpose is quite clearly to convince people just who Jesus was. For Mark, he is Christ, the Messiah. The whole book is a more detailed and developed presentation of that early Christian proclamation (see unit 16): the Messiah must suffer and die and rise again according to the scriptures;

Jesus has suffered and died and risen again; Jesus is the Christ.

The words 'Son of God' do not appear in some of the earliest manuscripts, which indicates that they might have been added as the Church developed its thinking about who Jesus was. The phrase only appears once in Mark apart from this and that is when the Roman officer comments on the way Jesus died (see unit 11).

There is a verse in John's Gospel which may well have influenced one of the copyists of Mark, and certainly sums up Mark's purpose in writing as well as John's – and Matthew's and Luke's for that matter: '. . . these have been written in order that you may believe that Jesus is the Messiah, the Son of God, and that through your faith in him you may have life.' (John 20:31)

Rome's tombs, a secret place of worship for early Christians

The following are simply suggestions. They are not intended to be a definitive list! Nor do they carry the sign of approval of any examining group. They are offered as ideas in the hope that you – or your teacher – may have some better ones! Please be sure to talk to your teacher about what you are planning to do. It is possible that there are snags which your teacher knows about but which you do not.

Musicals

Compare and contrast some of the ways in which Jesus has been presented musically over the years. Handel's 'Messiah' could, for example, be contrasted with Stainer's 'Crucifixion' and/or Rice and Lloyd-Webber's 'Jesus Christ Superstar'.

Groups

The various groups who are mentioned in the Gospel could be looked at in much greater detail. The Pharisees and the Sadducees are the two major groups but there are others like the Herodians, the Zealots, and the Essenes. You could compare and contrast these with religious and political groups in modern Israel. The Israeli Embassy will probably have some information on this; or you could talk to someone who knows the country well; or you could write to: Board of Deputies of British Jews, Fourth Floor, Woburn House, Upper Woburn Place, London WC1H 0EP; or Jewish Education Bureau, 8 Westcombe Avenue, Leeds LS8 2BS.

Peter

An in-depth study of Peter would make a very useful project. It would mean looking up all the references to him in the rest of the New Testament to start with. This would help you to discover the meaning and significance of things like 'Peter's pence' and the 'keys of the kingdom'. Then you would need to find out about the 'traditions' surrounding Peter which are not actually recorded in the Bible – things like how, where and when he died, etc. Another good approach might be to compare and contrast the attitudes taken towards Peter by a Roman Catholic, an Anglican and someone from one of the Free Churches. You may find that a local church is named after him. In fact, your finished project about Peter might be quite different from what you thought it might be at the outset. There are certainly quite a few different aspects to be explored about Peter.

Disciples

It would also be worth looking at the lives of some of the other disciples of Jesus. What they did later, churches that are named after them, etc. One interesting approach would be to study how they are presented in stained glass windows. You could produce a guide explaining how to recognize them and distinguish them etc.

Shroud Of Turin

The Shroud of Turin would be an interesting topic to follow up – not that you will come to any definite conclusions! It is claimed that this is the cloth that was used when the body of Jesus was wrapped up for burial. Ray Bruce and Ian Wilson have produced 'a resource book for religious studies' on the topic and 'The Silent Witness' is available on video. Ask your teacher for details of any further developments since the book was written.

Passover

The Passover is such an important background to the death of Jesus that further study would be useful. It would be a good idea to concentrate on the modern-day celebration. Purnell Book Centre at Paulton, Bristol BS18 5LQ will give you information about videos and booklets which are available from the Religious and Moral Education Press on the subject. You could also contact the two bodies mentioned under 'Groups' above.

Tour

You could design a tour of all the important places mentioned in the Gospel. This will mean finding out something about the present-day situation. Write some notes on each of the locations and design a brochure to advertize your tour! The Israel Government Tourist Office, 18 Great Marlborough Street, London W1V 1AF will be a useful source of information for this.

The Last Supper

A good project would be to see how the 'Last Supper' is celebrated in a variety of different Churches. It would be important to include a Catholic Mass and a Free Church Communion. If you were able to find an Orthodox Church that you could go to, that would make it really worthwhile. Alternatively, you could watch some videos to show you what happens. 'Eastern Orthodox' in the 'Believe it or not' series (produced by Central TV) will give you a good idea of the Orthodox Liturgy, while the first section of 'Aspects of Christianity' (RMEP) is a Roman Catholic Mass. Try to get hold of copies of the services so that you can follow what is going on. Stylite Publishing Ltd, 37 Salop Road, Welshpool, Powys, SY21 7EA can supply the Divine Liturgy of St John Chrysostom and the Catholic Truth Society, 38–40 Eccleston Square, London SW1V 1PD will be able to supply you with a Missal.

Temple

You could find out more about the Temple of Jerusalem, and the history of all the previous Temples, not forgetting the Tent of Meeting which was used in the desert. Find out why the original one was built, what it was like, whether there were any arguments about it, etc. Use the Jewish sources mentioned above for all these things. You could also find out from them if they think the Temple might ever be rebuilt and animal sacrifices begun again.

Holy Week

A detailed presentation of everything that goes on in Holy Week, from Palm Sunday to Easter Sunday, would be worthwhile. If you thought about it in advance, you could make some arrangements to go to one of the Services. This would mean that you could write about your own experiences and reactions – this is always welcomed by coursework moderators!

Death

The Christian attitude to death is worth exploring. It would mean talking to a local vicar, priest or minister, or (better still) all three, plus some Christians who have lost a loved one through death.

Funerals

Find out what happens at a Funeral Service. See if you can possibly arrange to get to one. They are mostly held during the week and it could be that at

some time in your two years' study one happens to coincide with your R.E. period.

Baptism

It might prove a bit easier to research the various forms of Christian baptism. Try to arrange to go to a service of believers' baptism at a Baptist Church if you can. Again, this will need some planning – they do not happen every week! The local parish church would be a good place to go for a christening, and you could compare and contrast this with what they do at the local United Reformed or Methodist churches.

Life After Death

Talk to some Christians about what they believe about life after death. Listen carefully to what they have to say, but do not be afraid to question them or talk to them about what you have discovered through reading this book. This could develop into a project where you could do a survey of different people's beliefs.

Suffering

You could do the same sort of thing with the topic of suffering. To start with, you might like to make a scrap-book of examples of suffering. If you do this, it would be a good idea to have a definite limit on the sort of examples you choose. 'Travel and tragedies' might be one, 'my town' could be another, and 'Africa' a third. But remember that just doing a scrap-book is not enough. Moderators like to see some evidence that you have done a good deal of thinking about it. Keeping asking 'why?' and recording the answer and you will not go too far wrong.

Chaplaincies

See if your local hospital has a chaplain. You could contact them and talk to them about their work. They might be able to take you on a visit to the hospital with them. Find out what other forms of chaplaincy there are. There are some full-time ones in large industrial companies, even in shopping complexes. Your project could be to assess how valuable the chaplaincy system is, ways in which it could be improved, etc.

Christian Organizations

The Sower – symbol of the British and Foreign Bible Society

There are a number of Christian organizations which are well worth a study. Most of them have national offices which you can contact and many will have some sort of local representative. There are too many to list all of them here. Try to choose something that has a direct relationship to what you are studying in Mark's Gospel. The British and Foreign Bible Society, the National Children's Home, the Leprosy Mission, or the Royal National Mission to Deep Sea Fishermen would be good

choices. Your teacher will be able to help you find one which is suitable and which appeals to you.

Healing

You may find it more difficult to explore something like 'The Church's healing ministry today', but it is certainly not impossible. That hospital chaplain, or a local priest or minister, or your teacher are good starting points.

Personal and Social Issues

There are a wide range of issues which you could explore, all of which are raised in part 4 of this book. Here are some of them:

Marriage and divorce
Food and fasting
Attitudes toward Sunday
Gambling
Giving to charities
Competition and rewards
Underprivileged people

You will need to talk to your teacher about this, however, because, if you are also doing a 'contemporary issues' type of paper in your GCSE, it might not be an appropriate topic for a piece of coursework under the heading of 'St Mark's Gospel'.

Films About Jesus

You may like to watch films like 'The Life of Brian' 'The Last Temptation', or one of the classic 'big-screen' presentations of the life of Jesus on video. It would be better to do this when you are well on the way to completing your study of Mark's Gospel. That way you will be able to write a good critical review of what you see.

Special Topics

You may be particularly interested in studying topics like the parables, or apocalyptic writing, or the miracles, or the way Mark makes use of the Jewish bible in his Gospel. These can be quite involved and complicated, however, and may mean your having to read books which you might find dull and boring if you are not already fairly deeply interested in these sort of things. Get some advice from your teacher as to how it might suit you!

'Let the children come to me and do not stop them'

INDEX